Robin,

On this Remembrance Day

We should never forget the brave men and women who fought and died to set the world free.

Kind regards,

H Michael

November 11/2023

The Day The Sun Danced

LESLIE MICHAEL

◆ FriesenPress

One Printers Way
Altona, MB R0G 0B0
Canada

www.friesenpress.com

Copyright © 2023 by Leslie Michael
First Edition — 2023

All rights reserved.

No part of this publication may be reproduced in any form, or by any means, electronic or mechanical, including photocopying, recording, or any information browsing, storage, or retrieval system, without permission in writing from FriesenPress.

Cover design by Creative Imagesetting

ISBN
978-1-03-916709-4 (Hardcover)
978-1-03-916708-7 (Paperback)
978-1-03-916710-0 (eBook)

1. RELIGION, CHRISTIANITY, CATHOLIC

Distributed to the trade by The Ingram Book Company

Dedicated to my grandson, Stefano whose quest for greater knowledge of history, religion and politics was the inspiration and the driving motivation that helped me write this book. It is my fervent hope it will stand him in good stead.

Introduction

During family gatherings, my 13- year- old grandson would ask me questions about history, politics and religion. There never was enough time to answer all his questions. I decided it would be better to write a book and present it to him as a gift. He promised he would read it, study it, research and fact check it. That was three years ago. As I kept pounding away at the keyboard, I realized I had written the history of the twentieth century and beyond. I was also stunned when I realized what I had written is very relevant to the current Ukraine War.

Long before World War I, World War II and the Cold War, there were other wars that could be grouped into one category – Religious Wars.[1] They raged for centuries across Europe that resulted in Christians slaughtering Christians. And we can safely assume it all began on the day in 1517 when Martin Luther hammered his ninety-five theses on the door of a Catholic Church. It was a declaration of war. He brought to the forefront the unbridled greed, the corruption and immorality of the Church. Luther was a Saxon peasant who became a monk and by his courageous actions, launched the

Reformation. He was an erratic genius, a raving anti-Semite and a man who hated Rome. By the time the Treaty of Westphalia ended the Thirty Years War, it had degenerated from a Catholic-Protestant conflict into a confused dynastic struggle and in the savage battles that ensued, Europe was laid waste. Towns and cities were burnt to the ground. Women were raped and people decimated. Many were burnt at the stake and others skinned alive. Serfdom was reinforced. Peasants were exploited by princes who held them in a degrading state of servitude. The pontificate of Urban VIII coincided with the decisive period of the Thirty Years War. He was guilty of unrestrained opulence and nepotism that included the enrichment of his family and desired the extinction of Protestantism.

William Shirer is the author of the monumental book, "The Rise and Fall of the Third Reich." It is based on the countless volumes of records of Nazi Germany that were found by the U.S. Armed Forces in various castles and mines. For years, those Nazi documents lay sealed in army warehouses, the U.S. government showing no interest in even opening them. Quite suddenly, during the height of the Cold war, the U.S. government was in a great rush to return them to Germany because America wanted that country to be the bulwark against the fear and dread of the Soviet Union and godless Communism. At the Nuremburg War Crimes trial when the U.S. Chief magistrate sentenced several Nazi war criminals to lengthy sentences and many to be hanged, they considered him insane and oblivious to the great threat from those godless communists in the East. However, William Shirer is to be commended that from whatever volumes he and his team could get their hands on and with little financial resources at their disposal, he and his dedicated staff came up with that brilliant and incredible history of Nazi Germany and how the world went mad.

Unfortunately, Mr. Shirer failed to include the role Christianity played in the rise of Adolf Hitler, a truly evil genius that led to World War II that brought untold sorrow and suffering to mankind. With great admiration and respect for William Shirer, I beg to state my case.

Chapter 1

Like millions around the world, I am deeply saddened by the turn of events in the Ukraine/Russia conflict and my heart aches for the innocent people especially the women and children who have been killed. One of the most heart-breaking and gut-wrenching scene shown on television was that of a young woman cradling a baby in her arms, crying inconsolably and saying, "My baby is dead. Kill me! Kill me!"

While we have been emotionally drained by this senseless slaughter, it must be borne in mind it is not the Aztecs who are brutally torturing and murdering people and then offering them up to their gods. These killings are being perpetrated by Christians who profess to be followers of Christ and who have been committing these unspeakable crimes for centuries. From the Latin-led Crusades to the constant, religious wars in Europe, to the 30 year-war, to both the World Wars, they have been slaughtering each other, fully convinced God was on their side.

Wars more often, than not, have always had a religious spark. The Crimean War [2] is one such conflict. Most people are aware of the historic Charge of the Light Brigade, the great battles fought and of course, Florence Nightingale, but are oblivious to the religious origins that left Russians angry and betrayed that Britain and France, two Christian countries, had joined forces with the Turks against Holy Russia. In the middle of the nineteenth century, a fight broke out between Latin and Greek Orthodox priests. It happened on Good Friday in the Church of the Holy Sepulchre in Jerusalem. Priests started arguing as to who had the right to lay their silk cloth on the altar first. The Western and Eastern Christians despised each other more than they hated the Muslims. Tempers flared and a fight broke out, turning the church into a free-for-all. Worshipers on both sides attacked each other with everything they could lay their hands on, including crucifixes. When calm was finally restored, dozens lay dead on the floor.

The middle of the nineteenth century also saw the growing hate and mistrust of Western Europe of Russia that, for decades, had been simmering. It inevitably led, across Western Europe, an expressed fear and hatred for that country. It became known as "Russophobia"[3] and it played on the fears, real or imagined of the Russians. Around 1836, thousands of pamphlets were distributed across Europe, detailing the uncivilized, barbaric and despotic "Russian Menace" that would in due course, threaten the civilization of Western Europe and further the aim of Russia dominating the European continent. They considered Russia to be the Asiatic enemy of Europe and desired to deliver a crushing blow against Russia, a country they absolutely loathed.

In 1095, Pope Urban II made the war against the infidels righteous for the men who took part in it.[4] He preached a rousing sermon calling on Europe's knights to free the Holy city of Jerusalem from the Muslims. This, he said, was God's will and the crowds cheered. Crusaders were given crosses that were blessed by the clergy and were promised spiritual benefits and forgiveness of sins. As they moved eastward, they unleashed the basest cruelties against the unfortunate Jews. They fell on defenseless Jewish communities, secure in the conviction they were in a holy war against the enemies of God. Many a Crusader wondered why he had to travel great distances to kill the infidels when they were right there.

Muslims were not the only targets. Crusaders captured and ransacked Constantinople. What they did was unforgiveable. They desecrated and plundered Hagia Sophia, often called Saint Sophia or the Church of Holy Wisdom.[5] It is considered the greatest and holiest shrine of the Orthodox Church. The savagery and disrespect of the Catholic Crusaders who bore the cross of Christ on their chests were unimaginable. What was shocking was the wanton sacrileges and desecration of the Church by Crusaders who had dedicated themselves to the service of God. They even stamped on gold and silver crosses. They loaded the precious goods of Hagia Sophia onto mules. The stolen sacred relics believed to belong to the Blessed Virgin Mary were sold to Catholic countries at absorbent prices. The most despicable act committed, was that of women of ill repute were paid to sing and dance at the main altar. Eastern Christendom has never forgotten those appalling days. Christians in the west do not understand the deep disgust and the lasting horror which the Orthodox Church viewed those events. They believe the Crusaders did not come in peace but came with a sword to sever Christendom. There is no doubt whatsoever that they succeeded.

The Albigensian Crusade was a military campaign initiated by Pope Innocent III against Catharism in southern France.[6] The Cathars were anti-materialist, calling for the return to the Christian message of poverty, chastity and obedience. They were against the scandalous lifestyle of the Catholic clergy. The Cathars who tolerated the views of others, were condemned as heretics and the pope declared all Albigenses to be eliminated. When attempts were made to bring the Cathars back to the Mother Church failed, Pope Innocent III then unleashed the Albigensian Crusade. What followed was one of the greatest massacres in the name of religion. Knights, in shining armour, who were promised indulgence, began the slaughter of the inhabitants of that region. A high-ranking clergyman is believed to have written the Pope, "The heretics were put to the sword and God's vengeance gave vent to his wondrous rage." Thanks to the Pope's generosity, the property of the dead was given to the Crusaders as "blessed" loot. When the Pope was asked about the innocent men, women and children who were slaughtered in the process, he replied that God takes care of his own.

In 1517, Martin Luther nailed his 95 theses on the door of a church.[7] It was a declaration of war and intended to bring to the forefront the unbridled greed, the corruption and the immorality in the Catholic Church. He was particularly outraged over the sale of indulgences that promised salvation. One of his theses fearlessly demanded an answer: "Why does the Pope, whose wealth is so great, desires to build the Basilica of St. Peter with money from the poor, rather than using his own money?" Luther was considered dangerous and a threat to the papacy. He translated the New Testament from Greek to German thereby making the Bible's teaching more understandable to the laity instead of hearing the word of God in Latin. In 1520, Pope Leo X sent a letter threatening him with excommunication. Luther responded by publicly burning it. He was excommunicated the following year. He was branded a heretic by the Holy Roman Emperor. He was arrested and his writings banned. It became illegal to shelter him and murdering him would not result in any consequences. It became the world's first known FATWA.

Chapter 2

On May 13th. 1917, the Blessed Virgin Mary[8] appeared to three peasant and illiterate children. Lucia, the oldest was nine years old. The Virgin appeared several times, spoke to them at length, showed those little children a vision of hell and entrusted them with three secrets. There was also a very personal request from the Blessed Virgin Mary for the conversion and consecration of Russia to her Immaculate Heart. She emphasized that if these were not fulfilled, that country would spread its errors around the world. It did seem very strange that no other country was named. What was even stranger is that the last apparition on October 13th. 1917, was accompanied by an unusual and terrifying event.

On that day, the sun seemed to dance in the sky. It rotated uncontrollably in a zigzag course and seemed to rush forward toward more than 70,000 people gathered in an open field. There was no fear, no screaming, no panic and no stampede. Yet no one present was adversely affected by the scorching heat. No photograph was taken even though there were several reporters and photographers present. Scientific instruments around the world failed to record this incredible and strange event of the sun moving erratically. People who were present gave varying, inconsistent and contradictory accounts of the "Miracle of the Sun" as it became known.

The Bible tells us, in the beginning, God observed the utter chaos below. It was a formless waste land and darkness covered the abyss while a mighty wind blew over it. In His infinite wisdom, He decided to create order out of chaos. He created the heavens and the earth. He said, "Let there be light!" And the sun was created to give light during the day and the moon to give light at night. The sun is stationary. The earth revolves around the sun. The moon revolves around the earth. There is absolute law and order in the universe. If the sun is to move erratically in a zigzag fashion, it would crash into the earth or the moon, not to mention other planets in our solar system. There would no longer be law and order and God's desire to bring order out of chaos would have been nothing but an exercise in futility! Millions of Catholics around the world believe it to be the "Miracle of the Sun." It has been more than a century and the Vatican has yet to declare it a miracle. It merely stated it was an "event worthy of belief." This blessed and wondrous woman was chosen through all eternity to be the mother of God. That message, in the form of a salutation and prayer, composed throughout the ages, was personally delivered by one of God most celebrated messenger – the Archangel Gabriel, when he said: "Hail Mary, full of grace. The Lord is with thee. Blessed art thou amongst women!" One wonders how the Blessed Virgin Mary, honored as the "Queen of Peace" could be biased and mean spirited as to single out Russia for conquest, conversion and consecration.

The first secret foretold the end of the Great War on October 13, 1917. That war ended more than a year later. The second secret foretold of the killing of a man dressed in a white robe. Most believers are convinced it referred to Pope John Paul II. But in the attempted assassination, he was seriously wounded but not killed. Lucia declared the third secret could be released after 1960. However, the Vatican published an official press release that year, stating it "was most probable the secret would remain under absolute seal." This triggered speculation the secret contained a prophecy of "nuclear annihilation to deep rifts in the Roman Catholic Church. During his apostolic visit to Portugal in 2010, Pope Benedict XVI explained to reporters that the interpretations of the third secret have a permanent and on-going significance and that it could even be extended to include the suffering the Church is going through as a result of the world-wide and rampant sexual abuse involving the clergy! Pope Benedict would eventually resign because he couldn't handle the filth in the Church.

Chapter 3

These apparitions with its anti-Russian message became a rallying Catholic war cry, and shamelessly used by the Catholic Church to magnify the "Red Menace." [9] It was given further impetus during the Civil War in Spain. In the early 1930s, Communism was considered the greatest threat to Europe and the Catholic Church. The clergy owned considerable land in Spain while laborers eked out a living on starvation wages. In 1931, the country became a liberal democracy that separated the Church and State. The Vatican feared the liberal government with all its freedoms would spell the end of the Church in Spain. Even though the Republican government was legally and democratically elected, the Church portrayed it as illegitimate and an enemy of God. This encouraged the justification of the Nationalist insurgency and defended its divine intervention for a country that had strayed from its godly path.

In 1936, Vatican Secretary of State, Eugenio Pacelli who would later become Pope Pius XII spent the entire duration of the U.S. elections in America. He, along with other high-ranking clergy, warned Roosevelt of the cold, political fact he would lose the Catholic vote unless he embargoed arms shipment to Spain. Abandoned by the West, the Republicans turned to the Soviets for military assistance. This played right into the hands of the Catholic Church and its portrayal of the Spanish Republic as a Marxist state. The war was now indeed a national Crusade to rid Spain of those godless Communists. From their pulpits, Priests spoke openly against the "Reds"[10] and denounced the Republicans as "Sons of Moscow." The conflict was supposed to be a civil war, but the clergy spared no pain in attacking the Soviet Union for its intervention, on the side of the Republicans, but were silent on the intervention on the side of the Nationalists by Nazi Germany and Fascist Italy. The horrific destruction of the beautiful and historic city of Guernica by the Nazi Luftwaffe, coupled with thousands of fascist troops from Catholic Italy, helped pave the way for a revengeful and brutal dictatorship under Franco. Thousands of Republican prisoners of war were killed and thousands more were forced to work on the construction of a monument to the memory of Franco in the Valley of the Fallen. It is a shame that in a Western European country, there stands a huge monument to the memory of one of the bloodiest dictators in history.

Decades later, President Ronald Reagan, a staunch anti-communist, paid tribute to the brave Americans who fought in the Spanish Civil War, even though they fought on the "wrong" side. This led people around the world to wonder if Hitler,[11] Mussolini and Franco[12] were the "right" side. It is hoped the current Pope will not evade the historic complicity of the Catholic Church with a brutal dictatorship that came to power, supported by Nazi Germany and Fascist Italy. The Church has also to explain why the Holy Catholic Church, when it considered itself in danger from the godless Communists, would turn to Nazi Germany and Fascist Italy for help. They further acknowledged there was a real danger to the Church but that was no excuse for siding with Hitler and Mussolini[13] and Franco.

Chapter 4

The persecution of Orthodox Serbs during World War II by the Ustasa in Catholic Croatia was carried out through executions in death camps as well as mass murder, ethnic cleansing, deportations and forced conversions. The largest concentration camp was the Jasenova[14] Concentration Camp that became infamous for its high mortality rate and barbaric practices where more than 80,000 Jews, Roma, children and anti-Fascists were murdered. It is believed Catholic Croatia was the only Axis puppet state to establish a concentration camp that was not run by the Nazis, but by the Croatians themselves. The camp commander, a doctor, was dubbed the "Croatian Dr. Mengele." Today, Serbia marks April 22nd as a public holiday dedicated to the victims of genocide and fascism, while Croatia holds an official commemoration at the Jasenova Memorial site.

By September 1943, the Nazi Wehrmacht was suffering unimaginable losses on the Eastern front and dying in the snow. In North Africa, they were dying in the burning sands. In Western Europe the Allies were pushing the Germans eastward. In Southern Europe, the

Allies had landed on the mainland of Italy and D-Day was just around the corner. Ironically, Italy, not only surrendered, but switched sides on September 8th – the day the Catholic Church celebrates the birth of the Blessed Virgin Mary – the one person whom Pope Pius XII believed would see to the defeat of the godless Communists, their conversion and the end of the Orthodox Church.

In November 1943, Pope Pius sent a letter to a convent asking the nuns to assist Jews fleeing Nazi persecution. It is the only known document which shows Pope Pius XII had sought to save Jews - and Jews were indeed saved. However, most of them had converted to Catholicism, or were of mixed marriages. Like Neville Chamberlain, the Church has been waving that piece of paper as proof of his saving Jews and in the fervent hope it will aid his canonization. Pope Francis has already brushed it aside, because for Pius XII to be canonized, a miracle has to be attributed to him. No such miracle has come to light. When he died, his body was so corrupted that at least one Swiss Guard fainted. The Church explained it was due to the heat of Rome. We learn from the Bible that holy men were thrown in a cauldron of burning oil and were not adversely affected.

Cardinal Todeschini, a personal representative of Pope Pius XII was entrusted with the most extraordinary task of disclosing to the devotees that the Blessed Virgin Mary had indeed appeared to Pope Pius XII. In 1951, thousands of pilgrims convened at the Fatima Shrine in Portugal. The Cardinal bravely faced the throngs of pilgrims and in a voice filled with emotion, solemnly disclosed that a note left by Pope Pius XII and found on his desk, stated he had witnessed the "Miracle of the Sun" -- not once, not twice, not thrice, but on four separate occasions as he walked through the Vatican gardens. It is believed he suffered from recurrent fits of depression and at times seemed deluded. Yet no records of his mental and physical health have ever been released.

It is not difficult to explain the Mariology of Pius XII[15]. He was entirely devoted to the Blessed Virgin Mary. As a young boy he would stop daily at the Shrine of the Madonna where he would pray and tell Mary everything. His lifelong devotion to the rosary, his frequent sermons on the Virgin Mary and his constant reference to her in his writings reflected his life had always been directed by her motherly love. He was obsessed by her warning about the Russian Menace and her personal request for Russia to be consecrated to her Immaculate Heart.

In 1929, he was made a cardinal by Pope Pius XI. He signed the Lateran Treaty with Mussolini whom he referred to as a man sent by God. On February 10/1939, Pope Pius XI died and Pacelli was elected as Pope Pius XII. Years later, he solemnly declared that the Immaculate Mother of God, Mary ever virgin, after her life on earth, was assumed body and soul into heaven. A day after declaring the Assumption of Mary into heaven, he expressed that this honor to her would introduce a spirit of penance and prayers for the conversion of Russia. Viewed in this light, the power of the Blessed Virgin Mary, an instrument of grace and intercession, took on staggering proportions.

Chapter 5

Communism was not the sole concern of Pius XII. He also agonized about Eastern Christianity and their conversion to Catholicism. He expected the Nazi invasion, joined by other European Christian nations in the invasion of the Soviet Union, to accomplish this goal and help Russian Christians with aid and conversion. He was also anxious to end the thousand-year East-West Schism that divided Christianity. Pope Pius XII was not Hitler's Pope. He believed Jews were the architect of their own misfortune. Instead of accepting Christ as their Lord, they crucified him, and Hitler was taking good care of them. Across the Blood Lands of Europe six million Jews and more than 25 million godless communists lay dead. It was his fervent hope "Operation Barbarossa" - the Nazi invasion of the Soviet Union, joined by countries in Central and Eastern Europe was a Christian Crusade that would wipe out the faithless Jews and those godless Communists from the face of Europe.

Hitler's horrid book, "Mein Kampf" is full of hate and dripping with the lust for power and revenge. Hitler believed the blood of the Jews is so putrid they are not even human – they are sub-human.

He cited passages from the Bible, noting that even Christ took a whip to them. He felt no sense of moral outrage at their plight. Any intervention on their behalf would draw the Catholic Church into an alliance contrary to the teachings of the Church. Hitler had planned a new world order. The whole of Europe would be ruled by the pure Aryan race that was destined to rule for a thousand years. The sick, the elderly, the physically and mentally handicapped were useless mouths to feed and would be exterminated. Others would be exploited and enslaved. They would toil in the fields to feed their masters and their land will provide more *Lebensraum* for the Master Race. Jews were considered inferior and therefore had no right to live. They too would be marked for extermination and Europe would be *Judenfrei!*

The outbreak of the Russian Revolution and the association of Jews with Bolshevism confirmed Pius XII nourished a suspicion and contempt of Judaism based on the belief Jews were behind the Bolshevik plot to destroy Christianity. In Nazi Germany, the concept of Jewish Bolshevism reflected a common perception Communism was a Jewish inspired and Jewish led movement seeking world domination. "The Protocols of the Elders of Zion" and Hitler's "Mein Kampf" clearly viewed Bolshevism as Jewry's effort to dominate the world. Historians denounce the concept of Jewish Bolshevism as deeply prejudiced. Law professor, Illa Somin called for the comparison of Jewish involvement in other communist countries such as China, North Korea, Cambodia and Vietnam where Jewish presence was virtually zero.

It must be remembered the whole world condemned Putin for the Russian invasion of Ukraine. Strangely, there is no evidence the world, including the Catholic Church, of condemning Hitler's massive and brutal invasion of the Soviet Union and the sole aim of "Operation Barbarossa" to wipe the communists and Jews from the face of Europe. Winston Churchill was pleased the Nazis were tied down battling the Red Army on the Eastern Front, thus making it easier for the Allies on the Western Front. Pope Pius XII was happy and pleased as the Nazi Wehrmacht rolled toward Moscow, victorious in one battle after another, Pius XII urged Catholics the world over to pray for a speedy realization of the Virgin Mary's prophecy at Fatima. In 1942, when Hitler declared that Russia was finally "defeated" he stated in a Jubilee message that it had fulfilled the Virgin's first injunction at Fatima and consecrated the whole world to Her Immaculate Heart. The conquering Nazis were at the gates of the enemy and soon the Soviet Union would be conquered and converted to Catholicism and the country consecrated to her Immaculate Heart. The godless ideology of that country, along with the Orthodox Church would be no more and Pius XII would be the supreme head of Christendom.

Chapter 6

But something totally unexpected happened. As the fury and might of the Nazi Wehrmacht smashed its way to one stunning victory to another on the Eastern front[16] and North Africa, German military commanders were basking in their glory. But as 1943 was dawning, Nazi troops were dying in the snow and bitter cold on the Eastern Front while others were dying in the burning sands of North Africa. Several Nazi generals and other commanding officers were openly humiliated and dismissed for their poor leadership. They realized the outcome of the war was now a foregone conclusion and it miraculously dawned on them they were really no followers of Nazism. They began to plot against Hitler, the ruthless dictator. They came to be known as the "Good Germans."

The West believes World War II was a conflict the Allies had won. The Battle of Britain, the storming of the beaches in Normandy and the Battle of the Bulge are images deeply ingrained in the minds of people in the west. They are remembered and recalled time and again as the Allied victory over Nazi Germany. But Russians recall it in a vastly and totally different light. For every allied soldier killed in battle, more than eighty Soviet soldiers died fighting the Nazis and the Fascists. More than 3 million Russian prisoners-of-war were starved to death. This was a blatant violation of the Geneva Convention. The siege of Leningrad resulted in the deaths of thousands. The soil of Crimea was soaked in blood as some 20,000 Russians were slaughtered, defending it against the savage fury and might of the Nazi Wehrmacht. The battles of Stalingrad and Kursk involved colossal clashes of steel and explosive power. Millions of men and thousands of tanks were locked in mortal combat in the greatest land battles ever fought. Nothing on the Western front matched the brutality and savagery of those battles. No Allied soldier fought on the Eastern Front. From the gates of Moscow to the Gate of Brandenburg in Berlin, more than 25 million Russians perished. When the dust finally cleared from the scorched earth, the dream of Hitler being the Master of Europe and the dream of Pope Pius XII being the Supreme Head of Christendom were forever shattered by those godless Communists.

The promises of Fatima remained unfulfilled. Russia was still a formidable force, more menacing than ever and much to the chagrin of Pius XII, it emerged as one of the greatest and most powerful military power in the world. Most people are of the opinion it was the blinding snow and the bitter cold that brought "Operation Barbarossa" to a standstill and then driven back. Few are aware of the pride and boast that nothing would stop the invincible Nazis from just overrunning the godless communists and the war would be over by October. Fewer still recall the "Miracle of the Sun" when it apparently danced and zigzagged across the sky and seemed to race towards the multitude gathered in a wet and soggy field that immediately dried up. No such thing happened on the Eastern Front. The Blessed Virgin Mary, with her incredible and immeasurable power did absolutely nothing. The sun did not appear or if it did, it did not ease the pain, the shock and suffering of the ill-clad Nazis and Fascists. They perished in the thousands and Russia not only remained unconquered, unconverted and not consecrated, they pushed the enemy back from Moscow all the way to Brandenburg Gate in Berlin.

The Cult of Fatima suffered a serious setback with the defeat of Nazi Germany. However, it was revived in 1947. Hatred against communist Russia was once more promoted. A statute of Our Lady of Fatima, depicting the Blessed Virgin Mary who hailed from the Middle East, as a lily white woman, was sent on a "pilgrimage" around the world, along with her message about the conversion and consecration of Russia and the fear if it weren't fulfilled, that country would spread its errors around the world. A document issued by Pope Pius XII called for the excommunication of Catholics collaborating with organizations attached to Communism. This document resulted in the largest excommunication in the history of the Catholic Church. No such document was ever issued against the Nazis. Hitler and Mussolini, both Catholics, were not excommunicated. Pius XII was so obsessed with the godless Communists and the Orthodox Church that he did not even care to address the medieval anti-Semitism that had for centuries raged in the Church and culminated in the Holocaust where six million Jews were ghastly exterminated. Racism against the blacks was ignored and the appalling conditions the indigenous people lived under did not bother him, even when it became an international eye sore. To this very day, the Cult of Fatima still lingers on. On March 25th, 2022, the day the Catholic Church commemorates the Annunciation of the Blessed Virgin Mary, Pope Francis consecrated Russia to her Immaculate Heart. For good measure, he added Ukraine.

Chapter 7

The West and the Soviet Union were allies in World War II. However, the relationship between the two had always been one of tension and suspicion. The West was always weary of the Soviets and their godless communism. Conversely, the Soviets resented the portrayal of them as the "Asiatic" enemy, culturally inferior and barbaric even though they had courageously fought a common enemy and driven them more than a thousand miles back to Berlin at a staggering cost of human lives and their infrastructure in ruins. They resented the refusal of the West to treat them as an equal and a legitimate member of the international community. During the war years, Winston Churchill, an imperialist and ever mindful of God, King and country had been so eager to keep the Soviets battling the Nazis on the Eastern Front that he yielded to most of the demands of Stalin at the Conferences in Tehran and Yalta[17]. Churchill felt confident Stalin would keep his word. At the Yalta Conference, the Allies – Roosevelt, Churchill and Stalin agreed on the policies for enforcing the unconditional surrender of Nazi Germany. The expressed and inflexible view was to ensure that country would never again be a threat to world peace. Nazi Germany would be disarmed. All military hardware would be destroyed and factories capable for producing weapons would be crippled. At the Yalta Conference under sparking lights, numerous toasts with sparking champagne were raised including one that Churchill offered to Stalin, emphasizing the West regards Marshall Stalin's life as most precious to the hopes and dreams of all. He further added the West had a friend and unlike Hitler whom Neville Chamberlain trusted and was eventually betrayed, Stalin was someone the West could trust.

At the conference, the question of the repatriation of Soviet prisoners-of-war, particularly the Cossacks held by the Allies was discussed.[18] The Cossacks were "adventurers or free men" who lived in the northern hinterlands of the Caspian Sea and the Black Sea. They had a tradition of independence and finally received privileges from the Russian government, in return for military service. The term also applied to peasants who had fled from serfdom in Poland, the Dniepe and Don regions where they established free self-governing military communities.

Soon after the launch of "Operation Barbarossa" the Nazis took control of large areas of western USSR. Promising good pay and working conditions they enticed the population to wrok in Germany. However, the roughly 70,000 Soviets soon realized that in Nazi Germany, Slavs were considered *"Untermencsh"* (Sub-humans.) Hitler justified this by convincing his staff that the existence of those people is justified only by their economic exploitation of the Master Race.

As the tide of ear turned, Nazi Germany was losing soldiers and military hardware at an alarming rate and the need to work in farms, factories and mines became critical. They resorted to brutal kidnapping of Soviet citizens. Thousands dies from disease and malnutrition. Those strong enough were sent to labour camps where they were worked to death. The huge losses on the Eastern Front continued and Germany forced the men to wear Nazi uniforms and fight for them. On the Western Front, the victorious Allies were closing in on Berlin. Thousands of Cossacks, in Nazi uniforms were taken prisoners. It was the wish of the Allies to remain on good terms with Stalin and hence they chose to hand over thousands of prisoners to the Soviet Union as a gesture of friendship. The Cossacks believed the British would have sympathized with their anti-communism. Unfortunately, they were totally unaware their fates were already sealed at the Yalta Conference.[19] Upon learning they would be repatriated to the Soviet Union, hundreds committed suicide. In a small cemetery near Lientz, Austria, lies the silent evidence of a wartime tragedy. There, 134 Soviet nationals lie buried. All of them had committed suicide. A similar incident occurred at Fort Dix, New Jersey where 154 Soviet prisoners-of-war, in Nazi uniforms were interred. The group attempted mass suicide, protesting the violation of the 1929 Geneva Convention for the treatment t of prisoners-of-war and the right to claim asylum. Historian Mark Elliot casts the repatriates as Pawns of Yalta who rights were sacrificed on the altar of secret diplomacy. Britain handed over 30,000. They packed them in trains and trucks and delivered them to the Red Army for repatriation to the Soviet Union where they were treated as traitors.

It could be argued that for Churchill there was a major concern. It was securing the return of all British prisoners-of-war who had fallen into Soviet hands as the Red Army advanced into Germany in 1944-45. British policies on their repatriation were directed by the fear that Stalin might hold them as hostages. It seemed that Churchill had a well-founded belief that if the British granted the Cossacks asylum, the Soviets would not return the British prisoners.

It was also maintained that since the Cossacks had fought for Nazi Germany, it was unreasonable to expect Churchill to sacrifice thousands of British prisoners-of-war to save the Cossacks.

S. M. Polkhy, in his book, "Yalta. The Price of Peace" stresses the need to set the Yalta Conference in its historic context as a war time summit when victory was close, but not yet achieved. He believes the Allied Statesmen – Roosevelt, Churchill and Stalin helped end the war and established conditions for a negotiated peace. He acknowledges their agreements certainly helped preserve the longest peace in European history. However, the agreements did involve the sacrifice of principles dear to the Western Statesmen, because the price was the subjection of half of Europe to a totalitarian regime. Soon after, Churchill, being Churchill, made the historic comment: "From the Baltic Sea to the Black Sea, an iron curtain has descended on Europe."[20]

Stalin could not trust Germany and was weary they would rise again and embark on another invasion of the Soviet Union to avenge their shameful defeat in World War II. He saw the advantage of buffer zones and the need to discourage other countries in Central and Eastern Europe from joining Germany again. With Stalin now firmly in control and just weeks after the capitulation of Nazi Germany, Churchill ordered his military advisors to come up with a plan that would see the Soviets driven back to Moscow. It was codenamed, "Operation Unthinkable."[21] It called for a massive ground and aerial offensive against the Soviet Union. It would be an armoured clash of steel, greater than the Battle of Kursk – the largest tank battle in history. "Operation Unthinkable" would involve thousands of tanks, backed by American and other allied forces. Yet the odds of the Allies succeeding were dismal. The Soviets had a far greater number of divisions and tanks along with an incredible amount of military hardware. The Allies had about four million men, mostly Americans who would soon be despatched to the Pacific to bring that raging war to an end. Defeating the Red Army would require additional forces and it was proposed rearming and retraining defeated Nazi Wehrmacht troops that would add to their military strength. The plan was highly explosive and controversial. There was outrage and horror at the thought of rearming former Nazi troops and a sense of betrayal of the Soviets who had been doing the lion's share of the fighting and who had endured untold sorrow, suffering and a staggering loss of lives. Allied military commanders realized that barring a nuclear war, they would never be able to push the Soviets back to Moscow. "Operation Unthinkable" was scrapped. Had President Roosevelt lived, he would have been appalled at such an idea as he hoped to continue a good working relationship with the Soviet Union. Winston Churchill, so lionized by the West, not surprisingly, was voted out of office in 1945.

Chapter 8

Millions of words have been penned about the Russian Revolution[22]. Historians and researchers are forever expanding our knowledge and the interpretations of events. There were several key factors that played out in bringing about the revolution. By 1917, Russians were sick and tired of wars – the Crimean War, the Russo-Turkey War, the Russo-Japanese War and World War I where almost two million ill-equipped Russians soldiers lost their lives on the battlefield and more than a million civilians perished. With hardly any men to work in the fields, food became extremely scarce. To make matters worse, there was an intense dislike for the granddaughter of Queen Victoria, Czarina Alexandra. Her husband, Czar Nicholas II was considered an ineffectual leader and whose advisers kept him in the dark about the awful prevailing conditions. And even worse, was the intense hatred and contempt for her constant companion and chief adviser, the "Holy Monk" Rasputin who wielded enormous influence on the Czarina. The Russians therefore welcomed the seizure of power by the Bolsheviks who seemed set on creating a new Russia that was free from social and class differences and who in addition, promised to bring peace, land and bread. Perhaps, it was Czarina Alexandra and not Maria Antoinette who said, "Let them eat cake!"

It is truly a crying shame, the West perceived Russia as an uncivilized and godless country that stemmed from the age-old "Russophobia" of the nineteenth century and reinforced by the "Cult of Fatima" of the twentieth century. It is a vast country that stretches across eleven time zones, making communication difficult. Russians are people of the East and not the "Asiatic" enemy of the West. It is the Christian East, historically steeped in the Orthodox faith. To consider Russia as uncivilized and barbaric is complete nonsense. Russia is the land of ancient culture. They produced incredible and spectacular architecture and wrote some of the world's greatest literature. One doesn't have to know a word of the Russian language to delight in its ballets and symphonies. Its operas are worth viewing for the spectacle and dramas. Russians take great pride in their cultural heritage. During the Soviet era, almost everyone went to the theater, the concert hall and the opera house to pay tribute to their great musicians and dancers who were trained from an early age with discipline and deep devotion. The Orthodox Church was always the soul of the Russian people and considered it as the only true Orthodox country in the world.

Unfortunately, the peasants were the majority who lived and toiled under the cruel and unjust yoke of serfdom making it extremely difficult for the poor to better themselves. People considered serfdom cruel and assigned the blame, not to the Czar, but to the ruling class – the nobility. The peasants thought it was wrong the nobles possessed vast tracks of land. A landowner could punish his serfs at his own discretion and even had the right to sentence them to hard labour in Siberia. The only thing a nobleman could not do was to kill them.

The peasants believed the soil belonged to God and all who toiled at it should enjoy its fruits. The idea of ownership was something they did not understand, but fully understood by the nobility.

It wasn't just the nobility, but also the clergy who understood the great benefits of keeping serfdom alive and well. It was their intent to instill in the masses, the religious conviction that their suffering will lead to greater eternal happiness. Their rousing slogan was: "Bear the Cross and win the Crown!" Therefore, it was in their continued interest to ensure the public believed in religion, and hence made no genuine effort to understand the real source of their suffering.

By the nineteenth century, Russia was weak – spiritually and economically. Oppression and injustice prevailed. People were branded as trouble- makers and anarchists for challenging the enormous privileges of the nobles and the clergy. Living through bitterness and despair, many turned revolutionary. It was difficult to believe in a God who allowed such sorrow, suffering, injustice and the suppression of a living individual. While some Russians thought the creator of the world was an evil God, many were of the opinion there was no God at all. The peaceful and unarmed protests of the peasants, based on simple slogans such as "Peace, land and bread" and demands for land reforms were ruthlessly crushed. In 1905, workers marched to the Czar's winter palace to present their demands. The Czar's imperial forces charged the demonstrators, ruthlessly killing and wounding hundreds. Czar Nicholas II was perceived as a weak ruler and what he did and what he failed to do, along with his incompetence and poor governance, gave way to the revolution that caused so much damage for Russia and the enormous suffering of its people. The Czar along with his wife Alexandra and their children were brutally murdered in the middle of the night and under cover of darkness. Their bodies, maimed beyond recognition, were taken to a forest and buried in a secret location. The Russian Revolution that followed was one of the most significant events of the twentieth century and had a deep impact on the entire world.

Chapter 9

It is true the Bolsheviks, in the middle of the night and under cover of darkness, brutally murdered the Czar and his family. They reportedly buried them in unmarked graves in a forest. That act of brutality has always been used by the West and the Catholic Church to portray the Soviets as godless, barbaric, evil and the Asiatic enemy of the civilized and Christian West.

During the French Revolution,[23] Catholicism was the official religion. However, just a few years after the storming of the Bastille, churches were shuttered down and religious worship greatly curtailed. During the eighteenth century there was little praise for the Church in France. It was condemned for its power, wealth, immorality and influence. Nuns were admired as they devoted their lives to care for the poor and the sick. However, the clergy were seen as useless. People complained the church was full of priests who served neither the Church nor the state. They were neither useful nor ornamental. They were absorbed with nothing but trifling matters, spending time in prayer, instead of marrying and reproducing for the good of the country.

The Church owned more than fourteen percent of all the land in France. Its churches, monasteries, abbeys, convents, schools and hospitals portrayed the wealth of the Church and dominance in France. The Church was allowed to collect tithes, but exempt from taxation on its earnings, while the poor were burdened with unjust taxation. They were convinced the sale of monasteries and other properties would help the country's finances. Church bells came down and were melted. Churches were converted into warehouses and even stables. Like Czar Nicholas II, Louis XVI was also viewed as a weak and ineffectual leader. However, unlike Russia's first family, who were brutally murdered in the dead of night and unceremoniously buried in a secret location, Louis XVI, his wife, Maria Antoinette and other members of the nobility were guillotined with pomp and gaiety while peasants cheered as their heads rolled into a basket. Yet to this very day, Russia is held in contempt and branded as godless by the Catholic Church and the fear and dread of the "RED MENACE" still hangs over the heads of western nations while the 14th of July, the day the Bastille was stormed, ushering in the French Revolution, is a celebrated as a national holiday in France.

Chapter 10

Despite the fact of being allies in World War II, the relationship between the United States and the Soviet Union was one of tension, suspicion and mistrust. Instead of being mindful of the fact it was the Red Army who, against unimaginable odds defeated the Nazis at a staggering loss of lives and greatly helped to set the world free, the Catholic Church continued with its Fatima Cult with its anti-Russian message. A statue of the Lady of Fatima depicting the Blessed Virgin Mary as the Lady of the Rosary was sent far and wide with the ever present anti- Russian message and the need to pray the rosary daily for the conversion and the consecration of that country to Her Immaculate Heart.

In the meanwhile, grievances came to the forefront and inflamed the anger, distrust, suspicion and enmity resulting in the Soviet expansion and control of Eastern Europe. This only served to fuel the fears in western countries of Soviets aiming to control the world. The Soviets felt justified of their actions because those very same countries they now controlled had joined the Nazis in the invasion of the Soviet Union. They needed a buffer zone like Poland – a land that had been historically used for centuries as a launching pad for the invasion of Russia. With the Vatican turning a blind eye, it was clear these Central and Eastern European countries had joined the Nazis and formed a "Christian Crusade" to push the godless communists into the Pacific Ocean.

The end of World War II saw the beginning of another war, "The Cold War."[24] The U.S. and their allies agreed the only defense against the "Red Menace" would be a policy of "containment." President Truman justified the plan because he truly believed America should assist people to decide their own destination and feared the starvation, the poverty and dislocation of millions across war-torn Europe would reinforce the appeal of Communism. This strategy gave birth to the "Marshall Plan" that would see America finance billions to support and rebuild the economy of Western Europe from the ashes of World War II. The strategy of containment also justified the rationale for an unprecedented arms build-up with the recommendation the U.S. would come to the aid of any country to contain Communism no matter where, no matter what the cost. Ironically, that threat was taking place right at home. A committee on Un-American activities began a series of hearing designed to show communist subversion in America was alive and well. It forced hundreds of people who worked in the movie industry and other sectors to renounce left wing policies. Hundreds lost their livelihoods. Writers, directors and actors were blacklisted. State employees were accused of subversive activities. Senator Joseph McCarthy led the charge and expanded the probe to anyone who worked for the federal government resulting in hundreds losing their jobs. As the hysteria of the "Red Menace" spread like wildfire, liberal college professors were targeted as well. People testified against their colleagues. Thus began McCarthy's dazzling rise to fame as the most feared communist hunter in the country. It was only a matter of time before Americans became so fearful of Communism[25] that they were sure there was a "RED" under every bed.

Chapter 11

Since the dawn of time, man has gazed at the moon with all its wonders. He has revered it, sang about it and generally mooned over it. "Moonlight Sonata" was followed by "Moonlight Serenade." There is a "Paper Moon" a 'Harvest Moon" a "Silvery Moon" a "Devil Moon" and Frank Sinatra wanted someone to fly him to the moon so that he could play among the stars. Even a cow jumped over it. It has spawned a thousand love stories, a thousand dreams and a thousand legends. Various tribes put their infants in the light of a full moon to give it strength and women drank water that the moon had shone upon to make them fertile. The moon is earth's satellite and is considered "Earth's silent Partner." It affects the tide, keeps the oceans in a perpetual motion and provides us with the four seasons. Even though the moon is 248,000 miles away, many young women were promised it. While Ancient Babylonians considered the moon a safe place to hide from their enemies, the Soviet Union viewed the moon in a totally different light.

The end of World War II saw the victorious Soviet Union with no bases in the Western Europe to launch bomber planes or other offensive weapons against an enemy. With the end of World War II and the emergence of the COLD WAR -- a confrontation between East and West became a dangerous game. This confrontation created two different worlds pitted against each other. One was the free world of the democratic, capitalist United States against the closed and godless world of the communist Soviet Union. They were the two most powerful nations and sought to outdo the other with the manufacture of weapons of mass destruction. It soon became a dangerous and deadly game to prove who was superior in technology and its ideology and who could, not only build bigger, better and more destructive nuclear bombs, but also to place them on foreign soil. While the horror and madness of the arms race continued, a new and unexpected frontier was thrown wide open. SPACE! With the capture of numerous German nuclear scientists, the Soviets decided to use Space[26] as a base to defend and attack.

The fear, the loathing, the suspicions and the dread between the Americans and the Soviets continued unabated. On October 4, 1957, a Soviet R-7 intercontinental ballistic missile launched Sputnik into space. It was the world's first satellite and the first man-made object to be placed into the Earth's orbit. It caught America totally off guard. It struck fear into the heart of America because of the overwhelming power of the R-7 missile that seemed capable of delivering a nuclear warhead onto the U.S.A. America was further terrified in 1959, when the Soviets launched LUNA 2, the first space probe in the race to the moon. In April 1961, Soviet cosmonaut, Yuri Gagarin[27] became the first man to orbit the earth, traveling in a spacecraft called VOSTOK-1. Twenty Soviet Airforce pilots had been selected to train for the first manned spaceflight, but it was Gagarin's calm demeanor, quick learning skills and a beaming smile that made him the favorite. It was also his cool and calm composure, his nerves of steel and self-control that secured his place in history as being the first human in space.

Apart from potential engine and equipment failures, scientists were concerned about an individual's ability to survive while in orbit. Soviet engineers soon developed a fully automated control system. As an extra precaution the pilot would be given a sealed envelope containing a secret code for activating the spaceship's manual controls. The chief engineer privately shared the secret code with Gagarin before the flight to save him the trouble of fiddling with the envelope in an emergency. The flight of VOSTOK-1 was a terrifying ordeal. A hatch that failed to lock properly was fixed at the very last minute. Upon completion of the flight and on re-entry, he observed flames outside his spacecraft. He was assured by mission control that was nothing to worry about. The craft was on a home-ward bound path and he landed safely in a field. He was flown to Moscow to a hero's welcome. He was hailed by Khrushchev and greeted by cheering crowds as a glorious triumph on par with the defeat of Hitler and the Nazis in World War II. He basked in international glory, visiting several countries to celebrate his historic mission. Gagarin's pioneering single orbit flight made him a hero, a darling of the

Soviet Union. The huge propaganda, the success of Sputnik mission and Gagarin's flight prompted one senior space official to comment, "We have beaten the Americans even though our country has not fully recovered from the scars, the wounds, the massive damage and the incredibly high loss of lives we endured while facing the fury and might of the Nazi Wehrmacht!"

It was later revealed two days before the blast off, Gagarin had penned a letter to his wife, Valentina sharing his pride in being chosen to pilot VOSTOK-1 but also to console her in the event of his death. "I fully trust all the equipment to function well. But if something should happen, I ask you, my dear, not to be broken and overcome with grief." Seven years later he perished in an airplane crash. We are told, she never remarried.

Chapter 12

The Afro-Asian Conference of 1955, hosted by President Sukarno, was held in Bandung, Indonesia[28]. "Non-aligned" third world countries from Africa and Asia gathered to condemn colonialism, racism and express their concerns, tensions and fears about the Cold War. It was not a Communist Convention. These nations preferred to stay neutral during the Cold War, with the belief they would be better off by not allying with either the United States or the Soviet Union. Speeches condemned colonialism and imperialism. All forms of racism were condemned. The assembly called for an end to the nuclear arms race. The antagonism between the Soviet Union and the United States had little to do with these countries striving for economic development, education, health care and better living conditions. They sought to avoid the Cold War between Communism and Capitalism. The aim was to ensure their own independence, sovereignty, integrity and security in their struggle against imperialism and to follow their own paths without outside interference. They had no desire to be dragged into allegiance to either of the two superpowers. The United States was appalled by the Bandung Conference. Secretary of State John Foster Dulles[29] had already equated neutralism in the battle against communism as an unforgiveable sin. For America, the issue was black and white: join the West in the fight against communism or risk being considered an enemy.

Declassified documents reveal American involvement in a brutal anti-communist purge in Indonesia.[30] Several thousand Indonesians were killed for their affiliation or for just harboring leftist sympathies.[31] Suharto took over and ruled as a dictator with full U.S. support. Halting the spread of Communism and bringing countries into its sphere of influence was the ultimate foreign policy. U.S. provided Suharto with full co-operation, and it became clear the U.S. would stop at nothing, even the deaths of countless civilians to achieve its Cold War ambitions.

According to an article in the Daily Mail, March 19, 2012, the fear and dread of the "Red Menace" was screamed across America like a war cry. According to documents some nine thousand Nazi war criminals escaped to South America, including Croatians, Ukrainians and other western Europeans who helped the Nazis exterminate the Jews and others. Of particular interest was the focus on the "rat-lines"[32] – the escape route that allowed hundreds of murderers escape though passports provided by the Vatican and supported by Bishop Alois Hudal.

The United States was not an innocent bystander. After World War II, U.S. counter- Intelligence-Corps recruited Klaus Barbie – the Gestapo Chief in Lyon, France as an agent to assist anti-Communist leanings. He played a major role in the deaths of thousands of French Jews and members of the French Resistance. "The Butcher of Lyon" was finally extradited from Bolivia and sentenced to life imprisonment for crimes against humanity.

With American support and financial assistance, the Iranian military[33] overthrew the government of Mosaddegh. He was a fierce nationalist. He attacked British oil companies operating in his country, calling for the nationalization of the oil fields. This brought him into conflict with the Shah, Mohammed Reza Pahlavi. British and the U.S. concluded Mosaddegh had leftist leanings and would surely drag Iran into the Soviet orbit.[34] The CIA began its covert operations along with pro-Shah forces. The CIA cajoled, bribed and threatened its way and organized a coup against Mosaddegh. The Shah assumed power and in gratitude signed over a great percentage of Iran's oilfields to U.S. companies. Mossaddegh was arrested and died under house arrest. The Shah became one of the most trusted head of state as American economic and military aid poured in.

SAVAK was the secret police that was established by the Shah with the help of the CIA. It was hated and feared because it tortured and murdered thousands of opponents of the Shah's regime. This was accomplished with brutality that included "scientific" methods to prevent death under torture. These included sleep deprivations, solitary confinement, nail extractions, electric shocks, sitting on hot grills, and mock executions. In 1978, anti-Shah and anti U.S. protests broke out in Iran and the Shah was toppled. In 1979, angry protesters seized the American Embassy and held the U.S. staff hostage for 444 days.

Patrice Lumumba was the first duly elected Prime Minister of the Democratic Republic of Congo[35]. The day's celebrations were attended by the King of Belgium, many dignitaries and members of the foreign press. The King praised the developments under "colonialism" referring to the genius of his grand uncle, King Leopold II. He also reminded the newly independent country not to compromise the future with hasty reforms and or to replace the structures that Belgium had built. This angered Lumumba and in an impromptu speech stated the independence of the Congo was not granted freely by Belgium. He further stated no Congolese should forget it was by fighting that they were able to win their freedom. It was a noble struggle that put an end to the humiliating slavery and savagery that was imposed on them by force and resulted in the plundering of their natural resources and the death of some ten million of their people. The European journalists were shocked. The western media lashed out at Patrice Lumumba.

A mutiny soon broke out, led by Mobutu, chief of staff. Lumumba appealed to the U.S. for assistance, but America refused. He turned to the Soviet Union. This led the U.S. to believe he was a communist. Records show the CIA ordered the assassination of Lumumba because a Soviet takeover scared the living daylights out of the Eisenhower administration. The ties to Moscow frightened Washington. Lumumba's fierce anti-colonialism and the prospect of a Congo supported by the Soviet Union and its expansion in Central Africa, unnerved the West. Lumumba had to be taken out. He was captured and brought to Leopoldville. Despite appeals for due process and the demand for his release and restoration as the duly elected head of the Congo, he was eventually murdered. To prevent people from honoring him as a martyr, all evidence was destroyed. His body was dismembered with a hacksaw and dissolved in acid. Mobuto was given a private jetliner and a full staff for his personal use. The money that poured in was used by Mobuto to buy luxurious villas in Western Europe. The only change Mobuto brought to the Congo was to change its name to Zaire.

The U.S. seems to have been encouraged by the methods used in Indonesia, Iran and Congo in dealing with left wing insurgencies. It continued funding operations aimed at impeding and overturning left wing aspirations. Chile[36] had its own duly elected government that negotiated major ideological differences. But it was affected by the Cold War. In the presidential elections, Salvador Allende, a socialist-communist candidate was duly elected. He promised his people a republic and said he would institute reforms that would be beneficial to the working class. During his term he worked to form a government along social lines while respecting democracy, civil liberties and due process of law. He was friendly with the Soviet Union. That scared President Nixon who wanted him out of the way as he viewed him as a threat to democracy in Chile and Latin America. He did not want another Fidel Castro coming to power in South America under his watch. He authorized millions for the covert operation that included the overthrow of the duly elected president by a Chilean military coup. In 1973, tanks rolled into the streets and fighter jets screamed above. Allende was refused safe passage out of the country. He went into his office and died under attack from his own armed forces. He was succeeded by General Augusto Pinochet, a brutal dictator who turned the coup into the bloodiest in the history of Latin America. Thousands of Allende supporters were tortured, murdered and transported to unmarked mass graves. Thousands disappeared. The U.S. offered military and economic assistance to the new ruler – the "Saviour of Democracy". On one occasion, Pope John Paul II joined Pinochet on the balcony of the presidential palace and together waved to the cheering supporters of Pinochet.

Chapter 13

Indo China[37] had become France's most lucrative colonial possessions. They justified their imperialism by calling it a "civilizing mission" – white man's burden. That was a façade. The real mission was profit and economic exploitation. They saw opportunities to enrich themselves by securing raw materials, cheap labor and to establish a strategic presence in South-East Asia. Soon armed resistance surfaced. In 1954 the French-held garrison in Dien Bien Pho fell after weeks of fighting the Viet Minh forces led by Ho Chin Minh. More than fifteen thousand French troops surrendered. The U.S. seriously considered sending military aid to support the French. In a speech before the senate, President Kennedy declared that to send men and materials into the jungles of S.E. Asia without any possibility of peace would be dangerous and futile. No amount of American assistance could conquer an enemy that was everywhere and had the sympathy and support of its people. During the presidential debate, neither Kennedy nor Nixon paid any attention to Vietnam. By 1961, with Kennedy in the White House, Vietnam's problems became his problems.

In the wake of the French defeat, it was agreed to a temporary division. The French would remain in the South and Ho Chin Minh would control the North. Accepting the partition as unavoidable but still pledging to halt the spread of Communism in Asia, President Eisenhower initiated a program of assistance to South Vietnam. President Diem had the full support of U.S. military advisers who trained and reequipped his army. Covert operations by the CIA bought off or intimidated domestic dissenters and kept Diem and the economy afloat. Beneath the outward success of the Diem regime, fatal flaws soon surfaced. Diem was a poor administrator who refused to delegate authority and was pathologically suspicious of anyone not a family member. His brother and close confidant, Ngo Dinh Nhu controlled an extensive system of extortions, payoffs and influence peddling. Many of his officials and police engaged in extortions, bribery and theft of government property.

President Kennedy[38] who took office in 1961 perceived Vietnam as a challenge and an opportunity. Kennedy accepted without question the so-called Domino Theory which held that a communist success in one S.E. Asian country would lead to the fall of others. Kennedy considered Vietnam as the cornerstone of the free world and would provide evidence of U.S. determination to meet the challenge of communist expansion. Ho Chin Minh was not anti-American. He was disappointed by the lack of support given his people in their struggle for independence. He made several requests for American aid and campaigned for freedom. The corruption and political promotions played a major role in the weakening of the South Vietnamese army. John Kenneth Galbraith warned the U.S. of the danger the U.S. would bleed like the French. But Kennedy had to show America would pay any price to assure the survival of liberty and democracy. In America the word "Communist" was screamed across the country like an Indian war cry. Republicans said the country was imperilled by communist infiltration not only in the government but also in universities and schools. Communism was the battle cry and campaigns against communism were organized by religious groups. Every communist was a potential enemy of the U.S. and only the blind failed to see the subtle communist invasion of the country.

Chapter 14

The Vietnam War[39] continued its torturous path of death and destruction. Diem, a devout Roman Catholic and fervent anti-communist eliminated any political opposition by launching military operations against religious groups – mainly Buddhists. As opposition mounted against his harsh tactics, Diem [40]increasingly blamed the communists. In October, 1955, in a referendum on the future of South Vietnam, Diem rigged the polls supervised by his brother Ngo Dinh Nhu and was accredited with a laughable 98.2% of the votes. His American advisors had recommended a more modest winning margin of 60 – 70%. Three days later, he declared South Vietnam an independent state with himself as President. He represented extreme nationalism coupled with autocracy and nepotism. He also ignored the fact the Vietnamese people were not godless Communists. They were Buddhists and trying to convert them prompted Khrushchev to compare it like trying to put a saddle on a cow! Beginning in 1955, Diem launched the "Denounce the Communists" campaign, during which time communists and other anti-government people were arrested, imprisoned, tortured and executed. He instituted the death penalty against any activity deemed communist. Thousands, suspected of being opponents of Diem were killed and thousands more, considered political opponents were incarcerated. Vice President Lynden Johnson who visited Vietnam enthusiastically declared Diem to be the "Winston Churchill of Asia." When asked to explain, he replied that Diem was the only boy the Americans had out there.

By 1963, there were about sixteen thousand American personnel in South Vietnam. The inept performance of the South Vietnamese army was exemplified when a major battle in January 1963 saw a small band of Viet Cong win a battle against a much bigger and better equipped force. Many officers seemed reluctant even to engage in combat. The forces of the South were led in that battle by Diem's most trusted general, Huynh Van Cao who was a Catholic and who had been promoted due to religion rather than skill. Americans concluded Diem was incapable of defeating the communists and seemed concerned with only fending off coups and had become paranoid after two attempts.

Discontent with Diem's policies exploded following the shooting of nine Buddhists who were protesting the ban of the Buddhist flag on VESAK – the birthday of Buddha. This resulted in massive protests targeting the discriminating policies that gave privileges to the Catholic Church. Diem's elder brother, NGO DINH THUC was an archbishop and aggressively blurred the separation between Church and State. THUC's anniversary celebrations shortly before VASAK had been bankrolled by the Government and Vatican flags were prominently displayed.

Chapter 15

President Kennedy was a Roman Catholic, a staunch anti-communist and a fervent believer in containing communism. In his first speech as President, he made it clear he would continue the policy of former President Eisenhower and support the government of Diem in South Vietnam. Kennedy also supported the "Domino theory" convinced that if South Vietnam fell to Communism, then other states in the region would follow. President Charles de Gaulle warned Kennedy the French were there for nearly a century and Vietnam would trap America in a military and political swamp and would bleed like the French. This was based on experience the French had at Dien Bien Pho where they were militarily defeated and left with a psychological scar on French policy. However, Kennedy had more daily contacts with "hawks" in Washington who believed that just a small increase in U.S. support for Diem would ensure success in Vietnam. The "hawks" were also strong supporters of the "Domino theory." Kennedy also had to show exactly what he meant when he said that America should "pay any price, bear any burden, endure any hardship and support any friend to assure the survival of success and liberty."

The forced moving of peasants destroyed hundreds of years of village life in South Vietnam and drove the angry peasants into supporting the North Vietnamese. President Diem who headed the South Vietnamese government was an autocratic, nepotistic head of state. He valued power more than the goodwill and wellbeing of his people. Diem banned political parties and refused to have a legal opposition. The country was plagued by greed, and corruption. He promised Americans political reforms, but never acted upon them. His style of leadership was keenly noted by the South Vietnamese who were becoming less and less enamored of their leader.

The most vivid scenes were staged by Buddhist monks who publicly set themselves on fire. This brought further attention to the despotic ways of President Diem and his religious bias toward his fellow countrymen. The monks accused Diem of religious persecution. Diem was a Catholic – a member of the Catholic minority and they accused him of suppressing their religious freedom. A member of Diem's government said, "Let them burn. We will clap our hands." Another said that he would be glad to supply them the petrol. Among those who saw the photo of a monk setting himself on fire, was President Kennedy. The breaking point for the American President came in August 1963 when Diem decided to use force to suppress the movement. That was the moment when Kennedy agreed with the CIA and opted for a regime change. He felt convinced Diem would never be able to unite South Vietnam and he had inherited a rapidly deteriorating situation in South Vietnam. U.S. officials began discussing a wide range of options. Chief among the proposals was the removal of Diem's brother, NHU who controlled the secret police and was seen as the man behind the Buddhist suppression and the architect of the NGO's family rule. The U.S. provided high ranking South Vietnamese military personnel with thousands of dollars to overthrow Diem. In early November 1963, Diem, along with his brother were brutally murdered on their way home after attending mass.[41]

When Kennedy heard the news, he reacted with utter shock. The murders were not in the script. The perceived participation of the USA in the assassination of Diem further deepened Washington's commitment to Saigon. America now had more responsibility for the South Vietnamese governments that followed Diem's brutal murder. The weakness of the Saigon government then became a major factor in the escalation of the war.

Chapter 16

Even though the city of Berlin was divided, people moved freely. However, East Berliners took advantage of the situation and professionals and skilled workers moved to West Berlin or West Germany. The Soviets were duly concerned with the brain drain and in 1961, the Berlin Wall[42] was erected. It completely cut off the freedom of movement between East and West Berlin. It was referred by the East as the anti-Fascist protective wall, while the West called it the "Wall of Shame," a monstrosity that kept free people imprisoned against their will. President Kennedy visited West Berlin where he gave his famous speech, *"Ich bin ein Berliner."* That phrase translates to: "I am a Berliner" Such phrases were used during the time of the Roman Empire that was the mightiest and greatest force in those days. To say, "I am a Roman!" was something to be extremely proud of. Unfortunately, that didn't stop more than two hundred people being killed trying to escape over the wall. Kennedy was still reeling from the Bay of Pigs fiasco and a humiliating summit meeting in Vienna where he was bullied and browbeaten by Khrushchev. Prior to that meeting, Khrushchev had made it clear the U.S. had lost its nuclear monopoly and presently, the Soviet Union had unspecified number of nuclear weapons aimed at Britain, France and Uncle Sam. He also compared the Allied occupied sectors of West Berlin as their testicles. If ever he wanted to cause the West pain, all he had to do was to squeeze them – and squeeze he did!

The year 1961 marked the 20th anniversary of "Operation Barbarossa" that launched the invasion of the Soviet Union by Nazi Germany. It is believed to be the most massive land invasion in history. They were joined by all countries in Central and Eastern Europe in a "crusade" to rid Europe of those dirty Jews and godless communists from the face of Europe. More than 25 million Russians would perish from that brutal and deadly onslaught. Memories die hard and the Soviets were in a foul mood. On October 27th, 1961, a senior American official, stationed in West Berlin and his wife, on their way to attend an Opera in East Berlin, were stopped at Checkpoint Charlie[43] by East German border guards, demanding to see his passport. The diplomat reminded the guards only Soviet officials had that right and that was in accordance with the terms and agreement regarding the postwar occupation of Germany. The diplomat and his wife were denied entry and unceremoniously turned back. Soon American tanks were rumbling to Checkpoint Charlie. Alarmed by the turn of events, Moscow ordered its tanks to the scene. American and Soviet tanks were now staring each other down barely 100 meters apart at Checkpoint Charlie. It was the most dangerous place to be. Just one mistake by a nervous soldier or a miscalculation by a commander would have, in the twinkling of an eye, resulted in a nuclear war. Thankfully, heads of State and military commanders kept their impulses in check and safely defused the 16-hour standoff.

The Day The Sun Danced

The thirteen days in October 1962 saw another confrontation between these two superpowers. The Americans blockaded Soviet ships from delivering nuclear weapons to Cuba.[44] The world held its breath as Kennedy and Khrushchev worked on a solution. Khrushchev made it clear if Kennedy feared nuclear weapons on America's doorstep in Cuba, so did the Soviet Union who faced the threat of U.S. nuclear weapons based in Turkey. Having approached the brink of nuclear conflict, both superpowers began to reconsider the nuclear arms race and took steps to agreeing to a Nuclear Test Ban Treaty. The Soviet Union agreed to take back the nuclear weapons that were destined for Cuba and the U.S. agreed the nuclear weapons in Turkey would be removed. Regarding the Berlin Question, the wall would remain. Kennedy later said that he preferred a wall to a nuclear war.

Later, in a letter to Kennedy, Khrushchev,[45] pointed out the fact both countries displayed wisdom and restraint in eliminating the military conflict that could easily have resulted in a nuclear war. He praised Kennedy for his courage because he was surrounded by hawks itching to unleash a nuclear war. He emphasized that in view of the now cordial relations, conditions were ripe to formalize an agreement on halting the testing of nuclear weapons. He noted America's participation in World War II but had suffered far less losses compared to the Soviet Union that suffered more than 25 million deaths. He also noted that America did not suffer the destruction of their cities and infrastructure. However, the Cuban Missile Crisis had knocked on the gates of America and the American people had inhaled the breath of nuclear war and have a clear realization of the threat looking over them if the arms race was not halted. He assured Kennedy the Soviet Union was not preparing for war when they delivered those missiles to Cuba. It was a means of defense and security of the Cuban people after the Bay of Pigs invasion and to deter any further aggression and to respect their integrity and sovereignty. Kennedy now turned his attention to national politics, planning to win the presidential elections the following year. He was concerned the backlash from the Civil Rights movement will cost him the south. Many were concerned if Kennedy was elected, blacks and Mexicans would take over the south. Right wing extremists brutally attacked the Civil Rights Movement and called integration idiotic and foolish. Thanksgiving was only a week away but that didn't discourage extremists from distributing leaflets bearing the front and side view of the President in the style of a wanted criminal. He was accused of being a coward for not standing up to the Communists. He was further berated for being blind as not see how godless and untrustworthy they were. They just could not be trusted to comply with any Nuclear Arms Treaty.

Kennedy had graciously accepted an invitation form Governor John Connally. He had planned to fly to Texas, make a few appearances and end the visit with a fund-raising dinner in Austin. The drive from the airport into Dallas was made in an open limousine. The police force had made the most stringent security detail to guard the president. The bullet proof bubble had been lowered so the president could stand more easily and wave to the cheering crowds. That pleasant afternoon would soon be completely shattered when shots rang out and President Kennedy slumped down, mortally wounded. A shocked and grieving America watched as images flashed across their television screens showing the unbelievable and unimaginable horror – the horrific, senseless, heart-breaking and brutal assassination of their beloved president. Newspapers around the world ran a photograph of a secret service agent jumping onto the presidential limousine in a desperate attempt to shield the president and Mrs.

Kennedy. That agent was willing to lay down his life to protect the first family from any harm.

The assassination of Kennedy[46] shocked the world. He was the youngest to be elected President and Commander-in-Chief of the Armed Forces. He was also the youngest to die in office. World leaders expressed shock, sorrow and utter disbelief. They ordered days of mourning and memorial services. The news of the assassination was flashed to the Soviet Union. It was greeted with incredible shock and consternation. In a "godless, communist country," church bells tolled for President Kennedy. Senior officials in the Soviet Union believed there was a well-organized conspiracy of the ultra-right wing in the U.S. They were convinced that the dastardly and cowardly deed was not the work of one man, but a carefully planned campaign to use the assassination to promote anti-communist sentiments. They were also of the opinion that Kennedy had paid the ultimate price for his peaceful co-existence and disarmament policies. They were also very fearful that some irresponsible general would launch World War III, and as a result the Soviet Union went on full alert.

In the meanwhile, Soviet officials were profoundly moved by the brutal assassination of the young president and wondered what would have been the outcome had there been a different president at the time of the Cuban Missile crisis. Khrushchev personally visited the U.S. Embassy to offer his sincere condolences. Madam Khrushchev did the same and warmly recalled, with tears streaming down her cheeks, of the memories of the Vienna summit conference and getting to personally know Mrs. Kennedy.

Startling as it may seem, White extremists in the American South were in a different mood all together. They seemed pleased they got that nigger lover and that any man who did what Kennedy did for the niggers, deserved to be shot. Blacks in the South openly wept on the streets, while whites showed no sorrow and pity and only regretted the president's brother, Robert Kennedy, the Attorney General had not been eliminated as well. This only showed the hatred and bitterness in the lives of racists and bigots. Kennedy was gone and Russia's genuine sorrow showed exactly what the world had lost. The memory of Mrs. Kennedy and her two children and little three-year old John giving that moving salute left broken hearts around the world. It was plain to see it was a climate of intolerance, hate and racism that led to the brutal, ruthless and calculated murder of a president and father of two small children who had, only a few months earlier buried his infant son.

Chapter 17

With the Soviet Union taking a commanding lead in the Space race, America was struggling to catch up. But it was the worst of times. The Civil Rights movement[47] was in full swing. Black men, women and children who marched peacefully were met with baton-wielding police officers and vicious dogs.[48] Martin Luther King's incredible and moving speech, "I Have a Dream" did not prevent his assassination. Riots broke out across the country and soon American cities were in flames. A five-year old black girl had to be accompanied by the National Guard to her Kindergarten class. A fifteen-year old girl, travelling on a bus, was arrested for not giving up her seat to a white man.[49]

In March of 2017, "Columbia," the official magazine of the Knights of Columbus, an organization of Catholic men, published a painting of the child Jesus in Joseph's carpentry shop. It is a beautiful work of art by Pietro Annigoni that depicts the child Jesus as white, with a shocking mop of blond hair. In an age of racism, bigotry, white supremacy and anti-Semitism, one cannot help wonder why the Knights of Columbus would print such a picture. It served only to encourage the fallacy of white Supremacy and the Master Race. Thousands of white people boasted about their blood being so pure and strong that they did not need the Covid-19 vaccination.

People have not failed to notice that in a Church, Christ is very often depicted as a white man hanging from the cross. One would never find the devil depicted as a white man with horns and a pitchfork. But one would always see Michael, the Archangel as a strong white man in full battle gear, ready to slay the devil, depicted as a hideous dark-skinned man. One cannot help but conclude it is extremely difficult for a white man to accept the fact it was a dark-skinned man who suffered and died for the redemption of mankind.

The firm belief that the lives of black people serve no purpose beyond subjugation is tied to white supremacy and the Confederate flag. Some two hundred years ago a line had been drawn across continental America. Modern day Americans find it difficult to understand the millions of enslaved African Americans in the south represented the greatest financial asset. The abolition of slavery would only result in the loss of property and the destruction of white supremacy. The slave owner will be degraded to a status of equality to the Negros. The people in the south believed they were doing the blacks a great favor. These people born and raised in a tropical climate would never be able to endure the cold and harsh winters of the north. They considered it merciful for them to be sold to the Southern planters where the climate was more favorable for their dark skin. The evangelization of the Negros was considered their most fruitful work because they would not have received salvation had they remained in the jungle waiting for missionaries to show up.

The blacks were not the only people to suffer. In December of 1890, about a hundred and fifty members of the Sioux were massacred at Wounded Knee,[50] half of them women and children. The incident was referred to as a battle, but in fact it was a tragic and avoidable massacre. It was unlikely the band of Indians who were in the process of doing their spiritual Ghost dance would have intentionally started a fight with the heavily armed cavalry. Historians believe it was a deliberate and revengeful massacre for the defeat of General Custer at Little Big Horn. It also served to end any organized resistance to reservation life where any Indian escaping, was hunted down like an animal. They did not even have the right to move freely in their own country. They were soon forced to adopt the white man's culture. They were required to learn English, wear western clothes, observe Christianity and abandon their traditional religion. The process of assimilation required the removal of thousands of these children who were torn from their mothers' arms and placed in Boarding/Residential Schools where the sole aim was to get the "Indian" out of the child in the belief that their Aboriginal cultures and spiritual beliefs were inferior. They also suffered cultural, physical and sexual abuse. They were forbidden to speak their language. They were also deprived of the love and care of their parents and communities. It was also wrong to separate the children from their rich and vibrant cultures and traditions. Thousands of these children died and their parents were not even notified. Suffering abuses as children made them powerless to protect their own children from suffering the same experience. With adult indigenous people in reservations and their children in Boarding/Residential schools, the land was empty. It is believed that 1.5 billion acres of land were seized from America's native people. It was based under the "Doctrine of Discovery" in the fifteenth century, whereby the ultimate sovereignty over any empty land belonged to the country of the Christian Monarch who discovered it.

Two famous explorers, Christopher Columbus and Vasco da Gama are to be remembered and commended for their intelligence, their skill in navigating uncharted waters and their courage to leave safe havens for unknown destinations. While the fame of discovering new sea routes and distant lands will always be theirs to claim, they unfortunately ushered in the age of colonization – and the arrogance and brutality of Christian Europe. In their unbridled greed, third world countries would experience the colonial power struggles of Western European countries as they fought their proxy wars on their soil. Their legacies include starvation, enslavement, racism, bigotry, plunder of their natural resources, the destruction of their art, culture and their great civilizations. It would forever be a reminder that powerful Western European countries took so much but gave so little in return.

The irony of forbidding the indigenous people to speak their native language was not lost. In World War II, in the Pacific theater, Native Americans were trained to operate a radio, identify enemy targets and send that message in their native language to control centers where swift actions were successfully taken. They were known as the Code Breakers or "Wind Talkers." [51] They contributed significantly to the American victory over the Imperial Japan. Their code was never broken. It would be several decades later, that President George Bush would pay a glowing tribute to them. Unfortunately, most of them were already dead.

Chapter 18

While the gloom and darkness continued, the moon kept shining brightly, brilliantly, mysteriously, intriguingly and captivatingly. So far and yet so close it. Like a flower in heaven and a goddess of the night, she beckoned, and man kept reaching out to her. Meanwhile, the Apollo program was making tremendous strides. In December 1968, Bill Anders, along with Jim Lovell and Frank Borman, commander of Apollo 8, took the very first color photograph of earth from outer space. It became known as "Earthrise" and became one of the most iconic photographs in history. It shifted the whole vision of space exploration and focused on earth, with its magnificence, wonders and beauty. It instilled a collective sense of wonder, awe and awareness of earth with no borders, no boundaries and reminded man that he is not only an inhabitant of this incredible and wondrous planet, but also its caretaker. During the Christmas season of 1968, the crew of Apollo 8 with millions around the world watching and listening, beamed back images of the moon and earth and took turns on Christmas Eve to read from the Book of Genesis along with a heartfelt wish for everyone on "Good Earth."

The mission became famous for the icon "Earthrise" image that gave mankind a new perspective of their home planet. Anders added that despite all the training and preparation for the exploration of the moon, the astronauts ended up discovering Earth.

Dr. Werner von Braun said everything had been done to assure the successful mission of Apollo XI and stated no manned space flight had been as carefully planned as this one. Dr. Mueller, associate administrator, answering questions, said that there was no way Neil Armstrong and Buzz Aldrin could be rescued from the moon if they got stranded there, even if another spaceship was launched immediately as the stranded men would have only 36 hours of oxygen on the moon. He added there were no suicide capsules on board in the event of a tragedy. He added the question of rescue had been discussed and space officials decided it would be money better spent on making the space vehicles work successfully.

A treaty had been signed by more than 70 countries that stipulated no nation shall make any extra-terrestrial claims no matter where the astronauts land. Furthermore, the U.S. will not regard the planting of the flag on the moon as ownership. However, they will place a plaque, signed by President Nixon and the Apollo crew bearing a map of the Earth with an inscription that read: "Here, men from planet Earth set foot upon the moon in July 1969 A.D. We came in peace for all mankind." Biblical verses from Psalm 8, written on a parchment sheet by Pope Paul VI would be placed in a sealed capsule to mark the landing site. It read: "When we behold the heavens, the work of your fingers, the moon and the stars which you set in place; what is man that you should be mindful of him, or the son of man that you should care for him?"

Chapter 19

Apollo XI blasting off on its historical journey. Signed by astronaut Eugene Cernan.

As the countdown began,[52] the restraining arms moved away to let the incredibly powerful Saturn V rocket hurl the shuddering, throbbing fiery 363-foot monster into the heavens. Atop that pillar of fire were three courageous men carrying the hopes and dreams of mankind. As Apollo XI streaked into the dark and frightening unknown at an unimaginable speed, the earth was revolving around the sun and the moon was revolving around the earth. Millions around the world held their breath as the spacecraft continued its historic journey to the moon. The date was July 16[th,] 1969. The time, decided by the inflexible laws of the universe was 9.32 A.M.

With all the necessary maneuvers successfully completed, the Command ship, "Columbia" docked nose to nose with the Lunar Lander, "Eagle." Columbia then broke away from the Saturn rocket, and with the Eagle in tow, continued its way to the moon. Neil Armstrong and Buzz Aldrin eventually made their way to Eagle, leaving Mike Collins alone in the command module. The Eagle separated from Columbia and the descent rocket was fired sending the Eagle down to the surface of the moon. The Moon landing was a feat of human ingenuity, dedication, endurance and nerves of steel and the finals step came down to two men in a spacecraft where anything could go wrong – and did. The landing site had been carefully chosen in the area known as the Sea of Tranquility that had been determined to be relatively flat. However, as the two astronauts made their descent, they immediately saw a problem: a large crater with boulders. It was the worst landing area for the Eagle and the entire mission was almost aborted. Armstrong calmly took manual control of the craft and steered it to a safe place for the touchdown. He had to work quickly as fuel began decreasing rapidly when he made that last minute change. He maintained his concentration under enormous pressure. His heart rate soared as he touched down with just seconds to spare. Failure to land would have been a hard blow to take. Just four days ago, the whole world had watched and rejoiced over a flawless and spectacular launch atop a pillar of fire. Now everything would have been lost for lack of a few more seconds of fuel. The time was 14.17 pm. EDT. The date was 20th July 1969. Armstrong then spoke -- words that men, for centuries, had only dreamed of: "Houston? Tranquility base here, the Eagle has landed!" Those words came clear, across 248,000 miles of space and the whole world rejoiced. They

The Day The Sun Danced

had faithfully followed the progress of the mission and realized they had lived through the greatest moment in history. Men were on the moon and that old devil moon would never be the same again. After putting on their bulky spacesuits Armstrong made his decent down the ladder to the surface. As his foot touched the surface of the moon, he uttered the most incredible and meaningful message, "One small step for (a) man; a giant leap for mankind." It was a humble America that did not gloat over the incredible and historic voyage that won the excitement, wonder and admiration of the whole world.

Staying alive on the moon required the world's most expensive suits that Armstrong and Aldrin donned on. It protected them since there is no oxygen on the moon, no water and no shade to shield them from the sun's radiation. They carried their own oxygen and air conditioning to withstand the temperature of 250 degrees above zero. They also had a meteorite shield to protect them from meteorites streaking towards the lunar surface. A plastic bubble helmet was attached to the neck of the suit. Their gloves were designed for maximum flexibility. An elaborate pack, strapped to their backs, provided electric power for radio communications. Together the suit and pack back weighed more than 190 lbs on earth. On the moon it weighed about 30 lbs. The world danced and celebrated the incredible and breathtaking event. Almost everyone was touched in some way by man's arrival on the moon as they watched the miracle unfold across 248,000 miles across space to confront and dazzle unbelieving eyes. On that Sunday, July 20th, 1969, when Neil Armstrong set foot on the moon and spoke those historic and moving words it became the most memorable words spoken since the day, more than 500 years ago, when a man screamed in utter joy: "Land Ahoy!" heralding the discovery of the new world.

For centuries, man had dreamed about conquering the moon in a mighty and powerful machine and stride triumphantly over his new domain. Here on the moon, man arrived in an ungainly spider-like machine which he fully well knew might not even take him home. Armstrong, joined by Aldrin did what any tourist would do – took a few pictures. The most significant factor was the heightened awareness of our man's existence. All astronauts spoke lovingly of their earthly home rather than boast of their country. Headlines around the world screamed, "MEN ON THE MOON." (Not Americans on the moon.) Buzz Aldrin, speaking in a calm voice, asked everyone, whoever or wherever they may be, to pause for a moment, contemplate the events of the past few hours and give thanks in his or her own way.

Colonel Mike Collins, the "third man" of the Apollo XI mission was cited for his brave solo lunar orbit while his comrades were the center of the world's attention. He was also commended for bearing up under the solitude of his lonely vigil. Not since Adam had a human known such solitude as Mike Collins became the loneliest man in the universe. After their tasks on the lunar surface were completed, Armstrong and Aldrin successfully blasted off from Tranquility Base, piloted the lunar lander to link up with the command module, rejoined with Mike Collins, jettisoned "Eagle" and headed back home to a flawless touchdown in the ocean.

Photograph of Apollo XI astronauts signed by Buzz Aldrin.

Former British Defence Minister, Duncan Sandys sent ironic congratulations to Dr. Werner von Braun, a man he tried to kill during World War II. Sandys was the man who masterminded a bombing raid designed to wipe out the Nazi V-2 rocket base from which von Braun was showering missiles on London. Sandys cabled the inventor of the V-2 "I am thankful that your illustrious career was not cut short in the bombing raid on Peenemunde, 26 years ago.

A well-wisher set up a placard by the grave of President John Kennedy that read: "Dear Mr. President. The Eagle has landed!"

And finally, a guy became $26,000 richer as the result of a bet he made that man would land on the moon and would return safely before the decade was over. The bachelor had made the bet with a bookmaker in 1964 at odds of 1000-1.

Chapter 20

In the meanwhile, here on earth, President Lyndon Johnson had increased the number of U.S. troops in Vietnam to more than 500,000 from the initial 16,000. In 1968, Richard Nixon was elected to the highest office in the land. He promised to end that conflict. However, in November 1969, the My Lai Massacre[53] by U.S. troops of more than four hundred Vietnamese villagers that included babies became public knowledge. It took a courageous American pilot to land his helicopter gunship between the terrified villagers and the American soldiers to stop the frenzied slaughter of the fleeing men, women and children. American commanders when told of this took no immediate action.

On May 04/1970, National Guards fired at student protesters at the Kent State University[54], killing four students and wounding nine others. One of them suffered permanent paralysis. Some three hundred students had gathered to protest the expansion of the Vietnam War into Cambodia. The fatal shootings triggered immediate outrage on campuses around the country. More than four million students took part in protests at hundreds of universities, colleges and high schools. They highlighted the immoral role of the United States in the Vietnam War. The end of the war saw the ignominious defeat of the mighty United States Armed Forces by little men wearing sandals and straw hats. More than 58,000 Americans lost their lives - a great percentage of them were teenagers.

In 1983, President Reagan launched an invasion of Grenada[55] over concerns about U.S. students there. He did not even initiate any dialogue whatsoever. The invasion was criticized by numerous countries. Margaret Thatcher privately disapproved of the mission. The United Nations General Assembly condemned it as a flagrant violation of international law. Reagan had made no attempt to negotiate with Grenada. His goal was to destroy a regime he suspected was planning to export terror and undermine democracy. It would have been easy for America to turn Grenada into a model of prosperity and thereby show democracy as truly great and beneficial to all.

The invasion of Grenada was codenamed "Operation Urgent Fury." It was neither urgent nor furious. Margaret Thatcher considered Britain as the legal authority in Grenada because the colony was still part of the Commonwealth and warned Reagan an invasion will be seen as an intervention in the affairs of a small independent nation. Internationally, the invasion was criticized as a rash and dangerous reaction by Reagan to the killing of American troops in Lebanon – a possible comparison to the massacre at Wounded Knee for the humiliating defeat at Little Big Horn. The invasion was launched because Reagan desired to raise U.S. prestige at home and in the armed forces where morale had fallen and the humiliating hostage crisis in Iran. Ronald Reagan came to office pledging to restore America's glory and looking for an excuse to flex the country's military muscle. He had sent marines to intervene in Lebanon's civil war that did not produce the quick military victory he sought but instead resulted in the death of 241 service men in a suicide bomb attack.

Many attribute the fall of the Berlin Wall to Reagan when he stood before it and challenged: "Mr. Gorbachev, tear down this wall!" People fail to realize the Soviet Union was already teetering and near collapse. The Russians would have torn down the wall themselves. Leaving it there would be a constant and dreadful reminder of the colossal failure of its ideologies.

Chapter 21

The turmoil in Ukraine emerged as it struggled to forge an independent path, torn between Western Europe and its longstanding ties to Russia since Catherine the Great. Russians view Kyiv, the current capital and once the medieval Kyivan Rus, as the birthplace of their nation. Millions of Russians and Ukrainians have family members in both countries. The idea of a Western-allied Ukraine was viewed as a security threat to Russia. NATO troops in Ukraine would drastically alter the military balance as NATO also has troops and weapons in the Baltic region that borders Russia. Rather than a war, the Russian military buildup was meant as a signal to the West of Russia's extreme displeasure with its desired expansion of NATO in Ukraine.

During World War II, Ukrainians hailed the Nazi as liberators and collaborated in the extermination of some 243,000 Jews. It is almost impossible to get Ukrainians to talk about Babi-Yar where they are alleged to have helped the Nazis round up more than 32,000 unarmed Jews who were shot in two days. As the tide of the war turned and the outcome was a foregone conclusion, Ukraine allied itself with the Soviets. They were not alone. So did Finland and Italy. Ironically, Italy not only surrendered in 1943, but had switched sides on the 8th of September – the day the Catholic Church celebrates the birthday of the Blessed Virgin Mary.

Ukraine is considered a mixed up, failed and corrupt Fascist state with millionaires owning considerable assets in Western Europe. It became obvious to Putin that NATO wanted that country to get one step closer to Russia who felt threatened and concerned about its security. In a recorded conversation between U. S. Assistant Secretary of State, Victoria Nuland and the U.S. Ambassador to Ukraine Geoffrey Pyatt were heard discussing their wishes for a Ukraine transition in which they hoped to see prominent opposition leaders. Nuland was also recorded in the same conversation saying, "F**K the E.U., referring to their slow-moving efforts to address the political paralysis and the looming crisis in Ukraine.

The country continued to grapple with the unbridled corruption and deep regional rifts that had impeded its path. Among Russia's concern is the wellbeing of some 8,000 ethnic Russians in Ukraine and felt it was its duty to protect them. It was Ukraine's ties with the European Union that brought tensions to a boil. President Yanukovych scrapped plans to formalize closer economic ties with the E. U. that offered 833 million Euros with conditions that Ukraine will institute reforms to clean up the country's corruption and instead accept the offer of $15 billion by Russia. This ignited countrywide protests that came to be known as the "EUROMAIDAN." Putin branded the protests as a western backed fascist coup that endangered the ethnic Russian majority in Crimea. The West has still to address this accusation. Does this indicate that Ukraine is indeed a fascist state and Putin is right when he says he wishes to denazify Ukraine? With Fascism raising its ugly head in the U.S.A.,

Poland, Hungary, Italy and other countries in Europe, there should be alarm bells going off, not only in Russia but around the world as well.

If Ukraine is an independent, sovereign country, they have the right make their own decisions without outside interference. Yet, when Ukraine opted to go with Russia instead of the European Union, violent protests erupted! In March 2008, the Ukrainian President sent an official letter of Application Action Plan, the first step in joining NATO, the North Atlantic Treaty Organization - an alliance that was formed after World War II to counter the threat from the Soviet Union and Warsaw Pact countries. Several Western European Countries formed the NATO Alliance. It was agreed any attack on any one of its members would constitute an attack on all. NATO Secretary General declared in a press conference that Ukraine would someday join NATO. President Vladimir Putin listed his grievances with NATO and considered Ukraine's membership a direct threat to his country, Months of Euromaidan Street protests followed Ukraine's refusal to sign an Association Agreement with the European Union in favor of deals worth more than $15 billion with Russia. President Yanukovych had the right to do that. Yet, he had to flee the country and in 2014 parliament voted to remove him from office. If Ukraine and the West do not address this issue, Putin has good reasons to accuse Ukraine of being a Fascist state. They abolished the Russian language from being used in law courts, making it difficult for an Eastern Ukrainian to defend himself in a court of law. They claim they are one country yet voted to accept the European Union instead of the Russian offer – a country they are more closely aligned with – historically and culturally since the time of Catherine the Great. Ukraine claimed they were closer to Europe than Russia. They seem to forget Russia is also European or was it the same "Russophobia" of the nineteenth century and the Fatima Cult of the twentieth century that viewed Russia as godless, barbaric, and an uncivilized "Asiatic" enemy of the West? Putin saw this as a threat to the safety and security of Russia. In 2014, he annexed Crimea that had been, for centuries the historical home of the Russian Black Sea fleet -- and the West howled.

The Italian annexation of Ethiopia in 1936 was accomplished by a decree issued by the King of Italy.

Joint resolutions of Congress were the means by which the United States annexed Texas in 1845 and Hawaii in 1898.[56]

Israel annexed the Golan Heights in 1981 because it feared for its safety and security.

Chapter 22
Austria

The world seems to have forgotten that in 1938, Austria was annexed by Nazi Germany[57]. As Hitler rose to power, his desire to integrate ethnic Germans into the fold became his primary goal. He delivered a speech before the Reichstag which was broadcast live and relayed by the Austrian Radio Network. It was aimed at Germans living in Austria and Czechoslovakia and he emphasized that the German Reich will no longer tolerate the suppression of more than ten million Germans outside its borders.

A referendum was planned in which the ballot was not secret. Austrians were prepared to vote. "Did they want to be part of Hitler's Germany – or not?" Some of the most vicious and dangerous Nazis had seen to it, that the answer to the question would be an unequivocal *"JA!"* Through bombings, threats, coercion, demonstrations, manipulations and subversion, the result was almost a hundred percent approval of the annexations. The rape of Austria succeeded without a single shot being fired.

The seizure of Austria plainly demonstrated Hitler's aggressive territorial ambitions and the failure of Britain and France to take any counter measures. Their lack of will only encouraged Hitler to further aggression. The Allies were committed to upholding the terms of the Treaty of Versailles, but their response was verbal and timid. No armed confrontation took place. Cardinal Theodor Innitzer declared "Catholics should thank the Lord for the bloodless way this great change has occurred and should pray for a great future." Several other Austrian clergymen followed suit. The president of the Lutheran Church greeted Hitler as the saviour of the three hundred and fifty thousand Protestants in Austria. The campaign against Jews began almost immediately. Jews were forced to wash away pro-independence signs. Their homes and business were broken into and looted. Jews were expelled from public life. The gathering storm roared along and soon ushered in a shattering Kristallnacht - a night of broken glass[58]. The storm did not abate. Instead, it roared along, picking up hate, bigotry, racism, discrimination and religious fervor that culminated in the Holocaust where people who professed to be followers of Christ, committed the most unspeakable crimes against humanity.

The saddest aspect of the twentieth century is how countries in Western Europe, considered to be civilized, God-fearing Christians, far advanced in science and technology, could be so hateful and murderous. The horrors took place on the continent considered to be remarkable in the flowering of art, culture and startling as it may seem the cradle of Christianity.

Millions of words have been written about the assassination of Archduke Ferdinand of Austria that triggered the First World War that left more than sixteen million dead. What is woefully lacking is the explanation of what caused that tragic event.

To put this in its proper perspective, it should be recalled that Article 25 of the Treaty of Berlin in 1878, permitted Austria-Hungary to administer Bosnia and Herzegovina that were inhabited mostly by Serbs. It was a region that would offer the most convenient and long-desired access to the Adriatic Sea. Despite protest, the annexation of Bosnia went ahead in October 1908.

The official visit to Sarajevo by the Archduke and his wife was also a celebration of their fourteenth wedding anniversary. It was indeed unfortunate they arrived on the anniversary of the 1389 Battle of Kosova. This aroused the emotions of the Serbs who took it as a personal affront.[59] The Archduke had brushed aside the warnings his visit was unwelcome and might be dangerous. Sadly, the assassins did not know that the man they planned to kill was sympathetic to their cause. Ferdinand would eventually inherit the Hapsburg crown from his aging uncle, Emperor Franz Joseph and the Duke had planned to give the Bosnian Serbs a voice in the Austrian-Hungarian government. A tragedy of events followed. On June 18, 1914, the Archduke and his wife were assassinated by a Bosnian Serb, Gavril Princip.

The Austrians viewed the assassination as a dastardly deed. They presented an unacceptable and deliberately provocative document to Serbia, relying on Germany who a year earlier, had assured Austria-Hungary of its support, should a war against Serbia, erupt.[60]

They relied on Germany to deter Russia from any intervention. The answer from Serbia was unacceptable. It seemed Austria was merely looking for excuse, and on July 28 1914, declared war on Serbia.

> Russia had a treaty with Serbia. It declared war on Austria.
> Germany had a treaty with Austria-Hungary. It declared war on Russia.
> France had a treaty with Russia and off it went to war with Germany.
> Germany invaded Belgium in August 1914.
> Britain had a treaty with France and Belgium. It declared war on Germany.
> So on and so forth!

What was really pathetic is the fact that the King of England, the German Kaiser and the wife of the Russian Czar were cousins. They were the grandchildren of Queen Victoria.

If it weren't so tragic, it would have been downright hilarious.

And the question that remains to this very day is: Was the assassin Gavrilo Princip, a hero or a terrorist?

Connecting Christians to hate, racism, bigotry and anti-Semitism is a subject difficult to discuss in a polite society. We tend to place the blame squarely on Hitler and his willing executioners.

When we think of Jews being forced to wear the Star of David, we think of Hitler. Yet, it wasn't the Nazis who initiated that. It was the Catholic Church.[61] The Fourth Lateran Council (1215 A.D.) renewed the Catholic Church's terror against the Jews: Documents of Vatican II (1963-1965) clearly states Christian princes must watch lest Jews exact too high interest of Christian debtors; baptized Jews may not observe Jewish customs; Jews may not appear in public during Easter week. Jews must give tithes on their houses and other property to the Church and pay a yearly tax at Easter; no Christian Prince may give office to a Jew under pain of excommunication; Jews must wear a distinctive dress from their twelfth year to distinguish them from Christians.

For centuries, Catholics, the world over, prayed the despicable Good Friday Liturgy for the Jews. They prayed God would take away the blindness of their hearts and accept Christ as Lord. And for centuries, Jews were blamed for the crucifixion of Christ. It began on Palm Sunday, when Christ entered Jerusalem triumphantly. His path was strewn with palm branches. Jews were hailing him, saying, "Hosanna! Blessed is he who comes in the name of the Lord! Blessed is the King of Israel!" (John. Ch. 12-13.) Here was a King who had no legions to command and had entered triumphantly on a donkey! This scared the living daylights out of Caiaphas and other members of the Sanhedrin. The Jews at that time had some autonomy. They had the freedom to practise their religion and celebrate their feast days. They were terrified that even this would be lost because of one man who claimed to be a King. Caiaphas then addressed the members, saying, "You have no understanding whatsoever! Can you not see that it better to have one man die for the people, than to have the whole nation be destroyed? (John. Ch. 11: 49-50.) From that moment on, they plotted to have Christ eliminated.

They succeed in bribing Judas to betray Christ and apprehended him while he and his disciples were in the Garden of Gethsemane. They led Jesus to the high priest, elders and scribes of the Sanhedrin. There, they questioned him and brought several witnesses to testify against Christ. They found none of those testimonies could be used to condemn Christ. The high priest then asked Jesus, "Are you the Messiah, the Son of the Blessed One?" Jesus answered, "I am and you will see the Son of Man seated at the right hand of the Power and coming in with the clouds of heaven!" The high priest on hearing this, tore his robes and said, "What further need do we have of witnesses? You have heard the blasphemy! What is your verdict?" (Mark. Ch. 14: 53-64.) Christ had condemned himself and the punishment for blasphemy was death. The next day, they brought Jesus before Pilate, the Governor of Judea, who wanted to know as to why they could not take him and pass judgement according to their own laws. They answered, "We may not put anyone to death." (John. Ch. 18: 28-32.) They were aware the people were hailing him as a King. This was a capital offense against Rome and the only the Roman authorities could impose the death sentence for treason.

After intense questioning, Pilate asked Jesus, "Are you a King?" Jesus replied, "It is you who say I am a King" (John. Ch. 18: 37.) For the second time, Jesus condemned himself. Pilate knew in his heart that Jesus was innocent, but Jesus had acknowledged he was indeed a King and had said so in the presence of witnesses. That was a grave offense against Imperial Rome and as Governor, he represented Rome. With extraordinary courage, he made it clear that he found no fault with this just man. He washed his hands as he did not want the blood of of an innocent man on his conscience. Nevertheless, he knew he had to do his job as the mob was shouting, "If you free this man, you are no friend of Caesar. Anyone who proclaims himself a King becomes Caesar's rival." (John. Ch. 19: 12-13.) Pilate then handed Jesus to the soldiers to be crucified. He nevertheless showed further courage by placing a placard above the head of the crucified Christ that read: Jesus of Nazareth, KING of the Jews. It was written in Latin, Greek and Hebrew so that all would know that was his crime. (Mark: 15:26) When the chief priest told Pilate he should not have written, 'The King of the Jews.' Write instead, 'This man claimed to be King of the Jews.' But Pilate sternly rebuked them saying, "What I have written, I have written. (John. Ch. 19: 19-22.)

Vatican II also stated it is true Jewish Authorities sought his death. Nevertheless, what happened cannot be blamed upon ALL Jews – those living at that time and Jews of today. It further stated Jews should not be presented as repudiated or cursed by God. Vatican II reminded all that Christ, battered, bruised dying a painful, horrible and ignominious death, looked down from the cross and said, "Father, forgive them for they know not what they do." (Luke. Ch. 23: 34.)

In his book, "The Holocaust: A Jewish tragedy" Martin Gilbert tells us that Holocaust survivors, returning to Poland to pick up the pieces, were greeted by children hurling stones at them. One wonders what those children were taught in their homes, in their schools and in their Church.

Chapter 23
Czechoslovakia

Vitus Cathedral in Prague.

In a speech to parliament, Hitler made a pointed reference to the millions of Germans living in Czechoslovakia.[62] Hitler driven by hate disliked that country. That land had been cobbled together as part of the "settlements" of 1919 after the Great War. The country contained deep divisions, consisting of several peoples forcibly brought together in the post war "rearrangements" brokered by the

Allies. The roughly three million Germans living in Czechoslovakia were a pretext for Hitler's intervention. The Czechs had their great Skoda factory with a high degree of engineering skill that could add greatly to the Nazi war-making capacity. The "Munich Crisis" saw several visits by British Prime Chamberlain[63] to try and placate Hitler to agree to some settlement, almost anything to avoid a war. England was ill-prepared and Chamberlain reckoned delaying the outbreak of war would at least give the Royal Air Force the opportunity to acquire more planes to challenge the Luftwaffe.

England's declaration of War on Germany in World War I saw all Commonwealth countries come to the aid of Britain. It was not clear if those same countries could be counted upon again, should a war break out over Czechoslovakia – an artificially created nation. Demands for chunks of that country seemed reasonable since so many Germans lived there. Incited by Gestapo agents, the Sudeten Germans demonstrated against their "Czechoslovakian masters" marching through cities yelling: *"Ein Reich! Ein Volk!! Ein Fuehrer!!!"* Hitler iterated several times his absolute determination he would not tolerate a small, second-rate and artificial country treating the mighty thousand-year Reich lightly. He reminded the West, the Germans in that country were neither defenceless nor deserted and the world should take note of that and furthermore, Czechoslovakia was a country that began with a lie. With no viable options, Chamberlain consented to the occupation of Nazi Germany of the Sudetenland. The Czechoslovakians were not consulted and felt utterly betrayed. With tears streaming down their cheeks, they sang their national anthem while Nazi soldiers marched triumphantly into Prague, their beloved capital.

Chapter 24

With the Berlin wall dismantled, the Warsaw pact dissolved, the Soviet Union in complete disarray and effectively disarmed, Russia posed no threat. U.S. Secretary of State, James Baker, made his famous pledge to Soviet leader Mikhail Gorbachev that NATO will not move an inch toward the Soviet Union. It was assurances given by several Western leaders to Gorbachev and other Soviet officials regarding the security of the Soviet Union. James Baker agreed with the Soviets that NATO expansion was unacceptable. They all understood and agreed it was not just for the Soviet Union but for other Central and Eastern European countries as well. It is believed documents exists that clearly state the policies of the West were not intended in separating Eastern Europe from the Soviet Union. French President Mitterrand and British Prime Minister Margaret Thatcher backed the numerous assurances. Margaret Thatcher even went further stating she desired that NATO should transform itself into a more political rather than a threatening military Alliance. She told Gorbachev the West must find ways to give the Soviet Union confidence and its security assured. Gorbachev agreed to a unified

Germany in NATO based on the assurances given him. He truly believed the future of the Soviet Union depended on its integration with Europe. Gorbachev assured his people the West was not threatening their security and had no plans to expand NATO eastward – not even an inch! Like Prime Minster Neville Chamberlain, waving a piece of paper that Hitler had promised "Peace in our time" he lived to be contradicted. There is absolutely no doubt he was aware the West had betrayed his country and they had broken a historical promise, even after being advised by their own people that the expansion of NATO would be a great march of folly. The Western media have been telling the world what a wonderful person Gorbachev was. They keep telling the world that Gorbachev was a peace-loving man, he set the Russians free and allowed thousands of Jews to immigrate to Israel. That does not mean he was a push over and would have allowed Ukraine to join NATO and see the security of his country in grave danger. This is very clear and something the western media fails to report is that Gorbachev strongly supported Putin when he annexed Crimea. It is obvious Western European leaders have forgotten that if it weren't for those godless Russian Communists, the whole of Europe would be licking Hitler's boots and speaking German and Europe would have been *Judenfrei*. Perhaps the only thing the West had in mind that was what U.S. National Security Adviser, Brzezinski said in 1994, that without Ukraine, Russia ceases to be an Empire and probably saw the opportunity to teach Russia a lesson they wouldn't forget.

[64]To summarize the situation, the West believes that Putin annexed Crimea because of a decades-old desire to resuscitate the Soviet Empire and the fear that he may eventually advance further into Ukraine, in addition to other countries in Eastern Europe. The West also believes the ouster of President Viktor Yanukovych merely

provided a pretext for Putin to seize Crimea. However, other sources believe this to be wrong. The U.S. and its allies share most of the responsibility for the crisis. The crux of the matter is NATO enlargement, the central element of a larger strategy to move Ukraine out of Russia's orbit and integrate it into the west were also contributing factors to the current crisis.

Since 1990s, Russian leaders have adamantly opposed the enlargement of NATO and in recent years have made it very clear they would not stand by while their strategically important neighbor turned into a western bastion. For Putin, the illegal overthrow of the Ukraine's democratically and pro-Russian President, which he rightly labelled as a coup that was backed by the West, was the straw that broke the camel's back. Putin responded by annexing a peninsular he feared would host a NATO naval base that would destabilize Ukraine. Putin's invasion of Ukraine should have come as no surprise. After all, the West has, for years been moving into Russia's backyard and ignoring Russia's pleas for a treaty that will guarantee the safety and security of both Russia and Ukraine.

Obvious nobody was thinking of the famous painting, "Guernica" by Picasso. It portrays the suffering brought on by the madness of war. It depicts screaming women, a dead baby, a dead solider, a bull, a gored horse and flames. Woman and children have often been presented by Picasso as the perfection of mankind. Any assault on women and children is directed at the core of mankind. Picasso lived in Paris during the German occupation. A story widely repeated is that a German officer asked him, on seeing a photo of "Guernica" in Picasso's apartment, "Did you do that?" Picasso responded, "No, you did!"

Chapter 25

The question is: Can Russia trust its neighbours? Memories die hard. They can never forget that Central and Eastern European countries joined forces with Nazi Germany in "Operation Barbarossa" [65] whose sole aim was to wipe the godless Communists and Jews from the face of Europe. Moscow sees the agreement of Minsk II as a guarantee to its central demand that Ukraine is never allowed to join NATO. Washington and NATO have already rejected that demand. Putin has warned, twice in a week, that Europeans countries would automatically be drawn into a conflict in which there would be no winners if Ukraine joined NATO. For years, experts had warned the expansion of NATO was risky. The leading voice was the late American diplomat and historian George Kennan who wrote in 1997, "Expanding NATO would be the most fateful error of American policy in the entire post-Cold War era. It would inflame nationalistic, anti-Western and militaristic tendencies in Russia and restore the atmosphere of the Cold War between the East and West." Adding to that voice was the late General Colin Powell who said America should not make Russia an enemy.

President Putin really does not want to resurrect the Soviet Union. Contrary to popular beliefs and fear mongering, Putin has no plans to expand westward. He is wise enough to know he cannot accomplish that because of the fact he would have face the fury and might of more than two dozen countries that are aligned with NATO. He is also aware that from the Crimean War to the Russo-Turkish War to the Russo-Japanese War to World War I and World War II, the Russian people are tired of war. However, he sincerely desires the safety and security of Russia and her people and to restore the Russian peoples' pride in their nation. The world was pleased that the Secretary General of the United Nations appealed to Putin, in the name of humanity, to stop the war in Ukraine. They were disappointed he did not make the same appeal to Zelensky or to President Biden and NATO allies to refrain from providing billions of dollars in sophisticated military hardware, thereby prolonging the war and the inevitable loss of lives, especially the women and children. He also failed to remind them the present crisis could lead Putin to resort to nuclear weapons and there will be no winners and that the DOOMSDAY CLOCK has been moved to 90 seconds to midnight. In the meanwhile, Pope Francis has not called the conflict in Ukraine an invasion. Instead, he called the Russian Patriarch a brother and is alleged to have said Russia was provoked because the West kept barking at Russia's front door. Catholics the world over were wondering what ever happened to the prophecy of the Blessed Virgin Mary who said that unless Russia was conquered, converted and consecrated to Her Immaculate Heart, that country would spread its errors around the world. Not to be outdone, on 25th March 2022, the feast day of the Annunciation, Pope Francis consecrated Russia and included Ukraine for good measure lest he be accused of being biased like the Blessed Virgin Mary who singled out Russia as the culprit who would spread its errors around the world.

Chapter 26

In July 2022, Dr. Henry Kissinger,[66] the highly regarded, respected and elderly statesman ardently pleading with the NATO leadership not to prolong the war and cautioned about the catastrophic consequences on the fabric of European stability where nuclear weapons might be an option and there will be no winners. He has been saying it loud and clear and at every opportunity he gets. It appears a fair number of NATO members are of the same opinion but unfortunately have refrained from saying it openly. A good number of them also think NATO made a blunder by not taking the advice from seasoned diplomats, writers and historians. Dr. Kissinger emphasized Russia is an integral part of European politics and its role cannot be ignored, undervalued and degraded. He refrained from citing the 19th century "Russophobia" and the "Fatima Cult" of the 20th century that were shamelessly used against Russia. He also refrained from mentioning the anti-Russian message of the Blessed Virgin Mary at Fatima that was used as a rallying war cry that spread the fear and dread of the "RED MENACE" and resulted in Americans believing there was a "RED" under every bed.

Dr. Kissinger also believes in the restoration of the situation where Russia maintains its control of Crimea and Eastern Ukraine that has been a historical part of Russia since Catherine the Great. He is of the opinion Ukrainian forces, despite the full support of NATO will not be able to push back the Russians, nor have the Russians the intention of moving further into Ukraine. He firmly believes the war has to end at the negotiating table, something Putin has been advocating since the rapid expansion of NATO toward Russia. They knowingly and deliberately ignored it, kept poking the bear and like a school yard bully dared Putin to invade Ukraine.

Chapter 27

Americans are of the opinion that Putin hates democracy. How democratic is America? Thousands of Americans fought and died in World War II to set the world free from fascism and tyranny. Yet, America – the beautiful, the land of the free and home of the brave was the target of a brutal and deadly assault by fellow Americans. The world watched in horror as wave after wave of misguided American citizens, like monkeys, climbed the walls of the Capitol Hill. It is the symbol of democracy, shining like a beacon for others to see and follow. Instead, the protesters smashed their way into Capitol Hill, leaving a trail of broken glass, broken bones and and broken bodies in their path. The death and destruction that followed horrified the world. The most terrifying aspect of the attack on democracy was that it came – not from forces without, but from the hate, the racism, the bigotry, white supremacy and anti-Semitism within. It boggles the mind Americans can be whipped up into such a murderous frenzy as to want to hang the Vice President when all he wanted to do was his democratic duty -- to certify the elections. If sixty million educated Germans could blindly follow Hitler, it shouldn't be difficult that Americans can also be led to believe that twenty children and six adults were brutally gunned down in the Sandy Hook Massacre and that it was staged by Jews, even when there were twenty six death certificates, twenty-six coffins and twenty-six funerals.

As the world contemplates the first anniversary of the invasion of Ukraine by Russia, we should recall that on February 20th, 1939, Americans held a Nazi rally in Madison Square Garden to celebrate the rise of Nazism in Germany. Inside, attendees numbering more than 20,000 raised Nazi salutes towards a large portrait of George Washington, flanked by Swastikas.[67] Banners carried messages like, "Stop Jewish domination of Christian America and "Wake up America! Smash Jewish Communism!" The national leader of the organization referred to President Franklin Delano Roosevelt as "Rosenfelt" and the Manhatten District Attorney, Thomas Dewey as "Thomas Jewey." He demanded that American people with American ideals should have their country returned to the Americans who founded it.

At the time of that rally, Hitler was completing his sixth Concentration Camp. Jewish Americans called attention to the fact that was happening in Germany, could happen in the U.S.

Today, the rallying cry of the extreme right is, "We will not be replaced by Jews!"

Chapter 28

The invasion of Ukraine has been called a war crime and Putin branded as a war criminal. Consider the firebombing of Dresden,[68] Germany. Before World War II Dresden was known as the "Florence on the Elbe" and considered one of the world's most beautiful cities because of its architecture and art treasures. The bombing of Dresden demonstrated the air power of the Americans and the British. The military value of the bombing did not justify the destruction of that beautiful city. Given the high number of civilian causalities swelled by the flood of refugees fleeing the Soviet advance in the East and critics have called the bombing a war crime. Why were they fleeing from the Soviets? They were fleeing because it was their countries that had joined forces with Nazi Germany to obliterate the Soviet Union. On the night of February 13, 1945, British bombers incinerated tens of thousands of people and the U.S. continued the bombing with more than 200 bombers. Most of the victims were women, children and the elderly. They were not just bombed to bits. They burnt to death. People who tried to escape the firestorm by jumping into the river were boiled to death. Bodies melted in the heat. People were reduced to ashes. The attack by the British and the Americans was just another awful tit-for-tat civilian bombing of the war. The Allies rained down hell on Dresden for the same reason the Nazis rained down hell on London and other British cities to terrorize and demoralize the nation. In that, the allies succeeded. But the morality of doing so, applies as much to the Allies as to anyone else. No one seemed to remember the words of Gandhi who said: "An eye for an eye and the world will go blind!"

Perhaps, the bombing of Dresden was to display the fury and might of the Allies and the Soviets would take notice. They did! However, one wonders if the Allies realized it wasn't the success of "Operation Overlord" but the colossal failure of "Operation Barbarossa" and the courage and tenacity of the Soviets who faced total annihilation from the Nazis and the Fascists and pushed the enemy back to Berlin. One wonders if the West realized how the Soviets, particularly the women who dug trenches with their bare hands in the freezing, blinding snow helped drive the enemy back.

In 1945, President Truman had casually mentioned to Stalin the United States had a new weapon of mass destruction. Stalin did not seem particularly interested and said he was glad to hear that and hoped the U.S. would use it wisely. It soon became known that Soviet intelligence knew about it as early as September 1941. Historians believe, apart from other reasons, the Truman administration decided to drop the bomb for political reasons – to intimidate the Soviet Union - and prevent them from profiting in the spoils of war in the Far East. In the process they massacred more than 200,000 innocent men, women and children. The bombing of Hiroshima and Nagasaki served to hasten the Cold War and the arms race that saw the United States and the Soviet Union vying to outdo each other in weapons of mass destruction.

The Day The Sun Danced

In Vietnam, the Americans extensively used Napalm (liquid fire) that caused a lot of collateral damage, as once the fire started, it was almost impossible to extinguish it. A napalm bomb could leave a vast area engulfed in an unquenchable fire. Such bombs dropped by aircraft resulted in countless civilian deaths. An iconic photograph shows children, particularly a naked, nine-year old girl fleeing. That little girl survived and in later years said napalm is the most terrible pain one can possibly imagine.

In September, 1941, the forces of Nazi Germany closed around the city of Leningrad,[69] initiating the most infamous siege of World War II, and according to Hitler's directive to erase the city from the face of the earth. It would last for almost 900 days and claim the lives of some 800,000 lives. That number of lives lost equals the combined deaths of the United States and United Kingdom in World War II. There is hardly a parallel in history for the endurance of so many people over so long a time as Leningrad stood alone against the savage fury and might of the Nazi Wehrmacht.

During the early stages of World War II, the Japanese anticipated the fall of Bataan. Within hours of the American surrender, about 75,000 American and Filipino soldiers became prisoners-of-war. It was incomprehensible to the the Japanese as how to the enemy could have surrendered with so many troops. They could not contain the hate and contempt for the, especially the Filipinos whom they considered an inferior race. As for the Americans, they considered them cowards for surrendering and lacking the will to fight.

They planned to march the prisoners a distance of some 65 miles to various prisoner-of-war camps in the Bataan Peninsula. It became known as the Bataan Death March.[70] They were given no food or water. Thousands died from the cruelty and brutality of their captors who starved, taunted and beaten. Soldiers who tried to help fellow prisoners who were too weak to march had their heads smashed with rifle butts. Many were bayonetted or beheaded. Dead bodies littered the ditches and rapidly decomposed in the scorching heat. Tears flowed in the darkness as they thought of their loved ones back home and the heart break that would follow when they receive a letter from the government informing them that their loved one was killed or missing in action and presumed dead. Historians tell us there is not a more sensitive and tragic subject than the Bataan Death March. It ranks as one of the most vicious and revolting atrocities of World War II and referred to as the Forgotten Holocaust. Japanese Emperor Hirohito had refused to sign the Geneva Convention regarding the treatment of prisoners of war. He was never charged with any war crime.

The Manshu Detachment 731, better known as Unit 731 was a covert biological and chemical warfare Research and Development of the Imperial Japanese Army during the Sino-Japanese War that continued through World War II (1937-1945).[71] In 1936, Emperor Hirohito issued a decree, authorizing the development of biological warfare. It conducted tests on people who were infected with infectious diseases. Amputations were performed without anesthesia. Victims included men, women and babies born from the systematic rape by the staff of Unit 731. Those who did not die from these experiments were murdered. Their bodies were sent to the morgue for further studies. Prince Mikasa, the younger brother of Emperor Hirohito toured Unit 731 and watched films showing prisoners being marched in open fields for poison gas experimentation on human beings. Unit 731 soon became known as the Auschwitz of the East.

After World War II, Japanese scientists who conducted those inhuman experiments realized the American interest in their data would give them a powerful bargaining chip. They knew fully well the files they held would be immensely valuable to the Americans as they would not carry out the same research and experiments using humans as guinea pigs. They also knew it would also be the top priority of the emerging and powerful Americans to keep that data from falling into the hands of the Communists. Furthermore, they realized that any public war crime trials would involve public disclosure.

The U.S. authorities dismissed the alleged atrocities as communist propaganda. They eventually decided that the scientific and military value of those inhuman experiments took priority over criminal accountability. Emperor Hirohito was never charged with any war crime.

From the Rape of Nanking (1937) to the end of World War II (1945) almost 200,000 women, mainly Korean and others from occupied countries were forced to work as "Comfort Women" in brothels run by the Japanese military.[72] It was a systematic sexual enslavement of women that amounted to crimes against humanity. During their enslavement, the women were beaten tortured, raped and their genitals mutilated in the process. Those who survived the war lived the rest of their lives in isolation, humiliation, shame, stigmatization and extreme poverty.

Emperor Hirohito was never charged with any war crimes. Decades later, President Nixon humbled himself before Emperor Hirohito and President Obama bowed before Emperor Akihito, the son of the Emperor.

Chapter 29

The Catholic Church teetered along, virtually drowning in the rampant, worldwide scandal of sexual abuses by the Catholic clergy and the disgraceful and disgusting cover up by the Catholic hierarchy. From the eastern shores of Australia to the Andes of South America, the sun never set on the sexual abuse of the Catholic clergy. It was further noted, in a Catholic newspaper in Vancouver, Canada, that, by the time young adults reached the age of twenty-five, some 83 percent of them had left the Church. Pope Francis was absorbing all the arrows and bullets fired by Traditional Catholics in a crude, rude and disrespectful manner. Pope Benedict XVI who resigned because he couldn't handle the filth in the Church, began criticizing and interfering in the papacy of Pope Francis, including his handling of Bishop MacCarrick. It eventually became clear that both Pope John Paul II and Pope Benedict XVI were fully aware of the sexual abuses of MacCarrick. They did nothing and shamelessly tried to shift the blame on to Pope Francis. This is the same Ratzinger who, as Archbishop in Munich, was aware of the sexual abuse by priests but did nothing about it. He has been hauled on the carpet for doing nothing about it. All he did was to offer his regrets. Likewise, when the abuses in Residential Schools in Canada, run mostly by the Catholic Church surfaced with the discovery of unmarked graves, all he did was to offer his regrets. Several bishops and archbishops offered their sincere apologies – but not Pope Benedict XVI. Traditional Catholics and other right-wing clergy demanded to know as to how many times, does the Catholic Church have to apologize. They failed to understand that only the Head of State can offer a formal apology. In due course, Pope Francis travelled to Canada and offered his sincere and heart-felt apologies.

With egg on its face and the Church bravely marching on, a voice in the wilderness was heard. It came from a young 22-year-old, Amanda Gorman who is a Catholic. This youthful Poet Laureate was chosen to write and recite a poem at the inauguration of President Biden. Her poem, "The Hill We Climb" captured the hearts of Americans and millions around the world. She describes herself as a black person, descended from slaves and chosen to recite a poem at the inauguration of Joseph Biden, the newly elected president of the United States of America and shares with us the hope, she herself would, one day, become president. As a child she had a speech impediment but refused to view it as a crutch, but instead saw it as a gift. Throughout her poem, it is obvious she recalled great people who spoke words of wisdom such as: "We cannot direct the wind, but we can adjust the sails!"

Her poem recognizes the scars and wounds of America. We feel certain she hopes Americans will remember the words of Nelson Mandela who said: "Courage is not the absence of fear, but the triumph over it. A brave man is not one who does not feel afraid, but one who conquers fear" and pleads to her fellow Americans to strive to bring about a country that is committed to all cultures. Listening to her read her poem we feel she hopes America will remember the words of Gandhi who said, "An eye for an eye and the world will go blind" and will see, not what stands between them, but what stands before them. They should lay down their arms so that they can put their arms around one another." She certainly had the great Rabindranath Tagore in mind, when he wrote: "Let me not pray to be sheltered from dangers, but to be fearless in facing them." And in her final and profound challenge she wrote: "Such is the hill we climb. There is always light, if only we are brave enough to see it and brave enough to be it."

Chapter 30

One person was brave enough, not only see the light, but to be the light, even if it was at the end of the tunnel, it was still a light. That person is Pope Francis.[73] His beautiful canticle, entitled, "Laudato Si" translated as "Praise be to you, my Lord" reminds us that the earth is our common home.[74] The harm we have inflicted upon her by our irresponsible use of the gifts that God has endowed her with, causes her to cry out in anguish. The long-standing tension between the Catholic Church and Communism did not in any way deter the Pope from condemning Capitalism and affluent nations taking for granted they can plunder the earth at will and ignore the cries of the poor as long as they can get their hands on their natural resources. They understand only too well how thrilled people are when there is something new to purchase and their shareholders are happy. He condemned the culture of prosperity that rules and not serves.

There are many who can find fault even with the Lord's Prayer. They complain, after decades of economic growth, global wealth, an explosion of higher living standards and productivity, Pope Francis wants to turn the clock back. They pathetically fail to understand that none of the above involves real charity. They also fail to understand the blatant greed that was involved, when in the last century, pharmaceutical companies had women parade as nurses to promote baby formula in Africa and other third world countries where there is no clean running water. They fail to understand there is a stone so heavy that even God cannot lift it. It is a man's heart that is so weighed down with unbridled greed, envy and lust for power. The golden calf has returned with the worship of money and an economy that is heartless and truly lacking in charity.

In his numerous speeches and volumes of writing, Pope Francis mentioned a pastor in South America who said his people were hurting due to a smelter factory spewing toxic gases.[75] Surprisingly, the only hostility came from the local people who feared unemployment more than the toxic fumes. The pastor talked about Christ who wanted to do good yet was hated, rejected and murdered. He linked the sacrament of communion with the words priests use to consecrate the bread and wine: "fruit of the earth and the work of human hands" The pastor had a simple question, "What if the fruit is polluted?"

People in poor countries have been drastically affected by wealthy nations that fail to respect the environmental rights of local people. Pope Francis emphasized, on behalf of the poor, international organizations should challenge businesses that care only for their shareholders. We seem to have forgotten that we, ourselves are dust of this earth. He sincerely hopes we will remember astronaut Bill Anders who took that iconic photo of "Earth Rise" from space and said astronauts had spent years in studying and learning all about the moon. Instead, they discovered earth in all its beauty and glory.

By 1834, every corner of Africa was conquered and colonized by western European powers that fought their proxy wars on foreign soil, plundered their natural resources, looted, raped and enslaved people. They stole Africa's greatest assets –human beings. The richest continent on earth became the poorest. In the final analysis, the Catholic Church under Pope Francis has deemed Communism[76] is no longer the enemy. The enemy now is unbridled CAPITALISM.

Chapter 31

The Ukraine War has a definite religious connection. Pope Francis was criticized for meeting Patriarch Kirill in Havana and immediately branded by Traditional Catholics as anti-Christ and a communist. These two religious leaders were doing their best to solve their religious differences that for centuries saw them slaughter one another. The Pontiff, after celebrating mass on Easter Sunday decried the war in Ukraine without mentioning Putin and the launching of the invasion. Instead, he called Patriarch Kirill a "brother" and urged prayers for the suffering of the human family, broken by violence, war and injustices. Both are pastors of the same people who believe in God, in the Holy Trinity and in the Holy Mother of God.

To understand the Orthodox Church, one must go back in time and consider that "Orthodoxy" means "right worship." It is regarded as the one church that glories Him with right worship and is the true Church of Christ. In the year 312 A.D. Constantine had a vision of the cross and he became the first Roman Emperor to embrace Christianity. He decided to move the Roman Empire eastward. Rome was too steeped in pagan rituals such as the burning of heretics at the stake to form any part of the Christian Empire. The plunder and desecration of Haiga Sophia, the Church of Holy Wisdom by Catholic Crusaders was seen as the ultimate insult to Christianity.

With the invasion of Ukraine and the increasing loss of lives on both sides, Pope Francis seems able to grasp and fully understand the situation. He is fully aware of the religious conflict between the Roman Catholic Church of the West and Russian Orthodox Church of the East. Russians view the Holy Land as an extension of their spiritual motherland. The idea of "Holy Russia" includes the Church of the Holy Sepulchre as its Mother Church. The assault on Hagia Sophia and the ungodly acts committed by Catholic Crusaders left an indelible scar on the relationship between the two churches that remain to this very day.

For years, Pope Francis has been in talks with the Russian Orthodox Patriarch Kirill with the aim of easing the tension, the animosity and hate between the two churches and had been making much headway. In December 2021, Pope Francis met with Ieronymos II, archbishop of Athens and all Greece and head of the Greek Orthodox Church. Pope Francis apologized to members of the Orthodox Church of Greece for the ways Catholics offended them. He said, "Here today, I feel the need to ask anew for the forgiveness of God and our brothers and sisters for the mistakes committed by Catholics. Worldly concerns poisoned us. Weeds of suspicion increased our distance and we ceased to nurture communion. Shamefully, I acknowledge this for the Catholic Church – actions and decisions that had little or nothing to do with Jesus and the gospel – but were instead marked by a thirst for advantage and power that gravely weakened our communion."

The meeting in Havana seemed to have paved the way for the Pope to visit Moscow. Observers were full of praise. Unfortunately, as the Ukraine conflict continues, that hope has drastically dashed and dwindled. In the brief visit to Kazakhstan, Pope Francis failed to sit down with Patriarch Kirill or delegates of Chinese President Xi. Russian officials stated that western countries, particularly the U.S.A. have failed in the path of dialogue. President Xi reportedly refused to meet with Pope Francis while they were both in Kazakhstan.

The Russian Patriarch is a staunch supporter of Putin, and Pope Francis made the cardinal blunder of referring to Kirill as "Putin's altar boy." It seems any further progress is now in tatters and doomed to fail as the Russian Patriarch is shunning any overtures by Pope Francis. The Russian delegation made it clear it stems from the policy of Pope Pius XII who dedicated his whole life in the pursuit of two fundamental objectives: the destruction of Communism and the Orthodox Church. Pope Pius XII claimed absolute power in the west and believed that power also extended to the east. The Eastern Church assigned to the Pope, a primacy of honor, but not the universal supremacy he regarded as his due and something he craved for.

In the meanwhile, the war between Russia and Ukraine has taken an ugly turn and Putin has warned it could easily turn nuclear and there would be no winners. The sceptre of a nuclear holocaust now rests on the shoulders of Pope Francis. He should keep in mind that more than a century has passed, and the "Cult of Fatima" is still shamelessly being used by the Catholic Church. Pope Francis appears to be blind or deliberately failing to realize that in World War II when The Nazis were at the very gates of Moscow, they failed to conquer Russia. The Blessed Virgin Mary did nothing. The sun did not dance. It did not zigzag in the sky, nor did it coming rushing toward earth, melt the snow and give those godly Nazis a chance to conquer those godless Russians. Instead, thousands died in the snow and bitter cold and thousands more of those Nazis and Fascists from Catholic Italy were dying in the burning sands of North Africa. Russia remains unconquered, unconverted and unconsecrated and much to the horror of Pius XII, that godless country not only pushed the enemy back but emerged stronger than ever.

Ever mindful of the promises of the Blessed Virgin Mary and Cult of Fatima with its shameless anti-Russian message, the Catholic Church thought it would be a great idea to consecrate Russia during the current conflict in Ukraine. On 25th March 2022, the day of the Feast of the Annunciation of Mary, Pope Francis consecrated Russia to the Immaculate Heart of Mary. Months have passed and that war is still raging. Millions have fled, thousands have been slaughtered, including innocent women and children – and the Blessed Virgin Mary has done nothing. Worse still, the spectre of a nuclear Holocaust looms bright and clear. People wonder if Pope Francis, on that day in March when he consecrated Russia, realized he was flogging a dead horse!

He should instead, humble himself and ask forgiveness for the sins of the Roman Catholics against the Russian Orthodox Christians like he did when he met with Ieronymos II, Archbishop of Athens and all Greece. That would pave the way to meaningful discussions and reconciliation.

It would most certainly reduce the tension and eliminate, to a great extent, the possibility of one nervous soldier turning that conflict in Ukraine into an all-out nuclear war – in just a heartbeat! And the DOOMSDAY CLOCK has been moved to 90 seconds to midnight!

He should also be mindful the Fatima Cult was hateful, disgraceful, dishonest, shameful, vile and evil and THE DAY THE SUN DANCED would be a day that will forever live in infamy!

The Day The Sun Danced

Epilogue

The cause of the Ukraine invasion by Russia dates back several decades.

U.S. intelligence had discovered Cuba was constructing bases to be used for launching nuclear weapons on America. President Kennedy certainly did not want weapons of mass destruction on America's back door, nor did he want to see the spread of Communism in Central and South America under his watch. Batista, the Cuban dictator and an American ally, had forcibly seized power in 1952 and had cancelled the planned presidential elections. The country moved to the right and Batista solidified his position with ties to the wealthy elite and the United States. In the process, he severed ties with the Soviet Union. Eventually as the Cuban presidential election rolled around, there was no one to challenge him! He was in due course overthrown by Fidel Castro and fled into exile with millions and millions of dollars.

President Eisenhower had set aside millions of dollars for the CIA's covert operations to overthrow Castro, including, we are told, of attempting to poison Castor's cigars. Americans even supplied the air power to bomb Cuban military bases. The plan also included the Bay of Pigs invasion involving Cuban exiles that ended in a fiasco. It was at the height of the Cold War and that invasion was a U.S. foreign policy disaster. It strained relations between the two superpowers and drove Cuba into the arms of the Soviet Union.

The Soviets had for a long time felt insecure with the large number of missiles based in Western Europe and Turkey. Khrushchev viewed the deployment of nuclear missiles in Cuba as a way of levelling the playing field and a means of deterring any further U.S. aggression against that country.

President Kennedy decided to place a naval blockade around Cuba hoping that the "quarantine" would prevent the Soviets from delivering more offensive weapons. He also demanded the removal of those missiles already there.

The world held its breath!

How would the Soviets respond? Fortunately, both superpowers recognized the horrible and devastating possibilities of a nuclear war and agreed to a deal that would see the dismantling of those weapons in exchange for a pledge, a promise the U.S. would not invade Cuba. In exchange, the Americans would remove their missiles in Turkey.

Despite the enormous tension, both superpowers earnestly sought and found a way to defuse the crisis. Promises were made and promises were kept. And the whole world heaved a huge sigh of relief.

Long before the fall of Communism, Churchill's personal physician reflected on the Yalta Conference in 1945. He noted it wasn't a game of wits between the United States and Britain against the Soviet Union, but Britain against America! Churchill, the great Imperialist, felt the power of Great Britain and the sway it held over the world was slowly but surely ebbing and noted with great concern the rise

The Day The Sun Danced

of the United States. He felt uneasy and flushed every time colonies were mentioned but did not bristle when sizeable chunks of Europe fell into the clutches of Stalin, resulting in Eastern Europe falling into the Soviet sphere of influence.

In the early 1990s, the Berlin Wall had come down. Communism had dissolved and the Cold War had been won by the U.S. without a single shot being fired. America was now the most powerful superpower in the World. Soviet nuclear weapons lay scattered across former Soviet Republics, mostly in Ukraine. The U.S. and Russia feared those offensive weapons would fall into the wrong hands. Along with Britain and Ukraine, the Budapest Memorandum was signed whereby those nuclear weapons in Ukraine would be sent to Russia for disassembly. It was not a treaty, but a piece of paper, full of promises that all parties made for the security and safety of Ukraine. It also effectively disarmed Russia. The Warsaw Pact that was formed to oppose any threat from NATO was dismantled. With Russia in disarray and struggling to find a path to its own destiny, it posed no threat to the West.

The 1990s was a decade that provided the U.S.A. with the golden opportunity to be seen as a great superpower, admired and respected the world over. Instead, it showed no respect, no gratitude to a former ally that had faced the fury and the might of the Nazi Wehrmacht. It stood alone, not only against the Nazis but also countries in Central and Eastern Europe, including Ukraine that had formed a "Christian Crusade" to wipe those godless Communists and faithless Jews from the face of Europe. No Allied soldier fought on the Eastern Front. When the dust finally cleared from the scorched earth, the dream of Hitler being the Master of Europe was forever shattered at a staggering loss of more than 25 million Soviet lives and its infrastructure in ruins. It was the good fortune of the West that the Soviets paid the entire "Butcher's Bill" for defeating Nazi Germany.

In 1994, the Clinton administration[77] insisted, not only in perpetuating the U.S. dominated NATO Alliance, but expanding the Alliance eastward toward Russia, ignoring the verbal and historical promise given the West would not encroach upon Russia – not even an inch![78] This was carried out despite spite of the fact that:

Russia posed no threat.

A historical promise was broken.

American diplomat and historian George Kennan, in 1997 warned, "Expanding NATO would be the most fateful error of American policy in the entire post-Cold War era." He further added, "It would have an adverse effect on the development of Russian democracy, inflame nationalistic, anti-western and militaristic tendencies and restore the atmosphere of the Cold-War to East –West relations."

Thomas Friedman, America's prominent foreign policy columnist, declared it the most ill-conceived project.

Daniel Patrick Moynihan, widely considered the most learned U.S. senator cautioned that America had no idea what they were getting into.

The West failed to heed Margaret Thatcher's words of wisdom that NATO should be changed to a political party instead of being a threatening military Alliance.

General Powell said America should not make Russia an enemy.

Recently, in July 2022, Dr. Henry Kissinger, the highly respected and elderly statesman, pleaded with NATO leadership not to prolong the war and warned the catastrophic consequences where nuclear weapons could be an option – and there would be no winners. He believes in the restoration of Crimea and Eastern Ukraine where Russia maintains control as they have been a historical part of Russia since Catherine the Great. He believes Russia is an integral part of Europe and its role cannot be ignored, undervalued and degraded.

Casting aside the advice of many, the West showed no kindness, understanding, sympathy or charity for the Russians. It was like kicking someone in the teeth, punching below the belt and striking a person when down. The West saw this as an opportunity to make sure Russia stayed down as an ineffective and insignificant third-rate military power and faithfully followed the advice of U.S. National Security Adviser, Brzezinski who said in 1994 that without Ukraine, Russia ceases to be an Empire. Ignoring the historical promise not to encroach upon Russia, the West began the expansion of NATO eastward. They explained the expansion will erase Stalin's dividing line, but that dividing line that had already been erased with the fall of communism. They failed to see a threatening military Alliance was not the right approach to extending democracies in the former Soviet Republics that were, already well on their way to becoming independent, sovereign nations. Critics noted it was the Marshall Plan and not NATO that helped the reunification of Germany that emerged economically strong and a loyal and dependable ally of the free world. They emphasized that if the expansion of NATO continued that dividing line of Stalin will reappear and it will be confrontational. The fall of the Soviet Union was a time when an enlightened, powerful and compassionate America could have greatly helped Russia's integration into the democratic West. However, the Clinton administration embarked on a menacing and arrogant policy that paved the way to a new Cold War where the deployment of nuclear weapons looms as large as life and has the means of extinguishing life on earth.

President Yeltsin and other Russian leaders opposed the expansion and viewed it with great alarm as isolating Russia from Europe.

In later years, Putin had, for two decades been echoing the same concern and feared for the safety and security of his country. It fell on deaf ears – until Ukraine expressed its desire to join NATO. Putin repeatedly urged for a treaty that would guarantee the safety and security of both Ukraine and Russia. The straw that broke the camel's back was when Ukraine, as an independent and sovereign nation, chose to accept the offer from Russia instead of the one offered by the European Union. Violence erupted, riots tore the country apart and people were killed. Putin branded it as a coup backed by the west. Critics blamed the Obama administration for encouraging and assisting demonstrators to overthrow Ukraine's elected, pro-Russian president. In 2014, Putin responded by annexing Crimea, the home base for Russia's Black Sea fleet.

Pleas to negotiate a treaty that guarantees Ukraine will not be a member of NATO failed and Russia amassed a formidable military presence on the Ukrainian border with the threat of an invasion. The West ignored that, considering it a bluff. Putin invaded. The West vowed to impose numerous sanctions that would turn the Russian rouble into rubble. As hostilities continued, it has become evident it is Ukraine that has turned to rubble. Millions of Ukrainians have fled, innocent women and children have been killed and Zelensky continues to seek membership in NATO. He doesn't seem to understand that hell will freeze, and the world will end before that materializes. Putin wants his "pound of flesh." He will get it at any cost because he has now reached the point of no return – and China will not stand by idly and watch America take control of Ukraine and install nuclear weapons at its front door.

Recently, Finland became the latest country to be a member of NATO and would soon be joined by Sweden. Glancing at a map of the Europe one cannot fail to see that in the north there are the

Baltic counties, Norway, Finland and soon to be Sweden in the powerful NATO Western Alliance. With the exception of Ukraine, all countries west of it are also members of NATO. Looking eastward, there is South Korea and Japan with formidable American forces stationed there. Like Indians, circling the wagons, the West has surrounded Russia and ready for the kill. It would be interesting to know what Zelensky would think, say or do, if Ukraine was surrounded by hostile nations.

March 23rd 2023 marked the first anniversary of the consecration of Russia to the Immaculate Heart of Mary by Pope Francis. And once again, Catholics around the world were being reminded, for the last hundred years, about the need for the conquest, conversion and consecration of godless Russia to Her Immaculate Heart.

That date, March 25th was chosen because it is the day when the Archangel Gabriel, one of the most celebrated angels in heaven, appeared to Mary and delivered the most startling message the world has ever known. His extraordinary salutation was followed by words of praise for Mary who was full of grace, blessed among women and chosen to be the mother of God.

It was also the fulfillment of God's promise. Eons ago, in the Garden of Eden, after the fall of our first parents, He promised to send a redeemer to save mankind. It is also the most beautiful story of a man's love for his wife. When Adam saw Eve by the tree with the half-eaten apple in her hand, a sword pierced his heart for he knew at that very moment Eve had become mortal and she would die alone. He loved her very much. What followed was truly an act of love. He took the forbidden fruit from her hand and bit into it.

The Story did not end there. After the departure of Archangel Gabriel, Mary had to tell Joseph to whom she was betrothed, that she was going to have a baby! He was in a state of total shock. How could something, so beautiful, go so terribly wrong! His whole life had been turned upside down. He could scarcely believe Mary's words, "I am with child!" He did not and could not understand Mary's explanation. How could God choose a woman to be the mother of His Son, when she was already spoken for? Yes, she had been unfaithful. She had betrayed him! Fear and dread seized him as he knew what the penalty for adultery was. Stoning!

But he was an honourable man. He would marry her. He was, after all, betrothed to her. That marriage would save her from the harsh realities of the law. It would save her from being stoned for adultery. He would then quietly divorce her. But God had other plans. In a fitful sleep, an angel appeared to Joseph and told him not to be afraid and to take Mary as his wife. The Angel then explained to him that the child had been conceived by the Holy Spirit and that Child would be the one to save mankind. Joseph still loved Mary and no longer doubted what she had told him.

In Mary's canticle, she proclaims the greatness of the Lord and her spirit rejoices in God, her saviour and that the Almighty had done great things to her and holy is His name. Millions around the world have so much love and devotion to the Holy Mother of God. This book has been written in defense of the Blessed Virgin Mary. It is truly inconceivable that such a kind, gentle, loving woman would be so mean-spirited as to single out Russia as the evil and godless enemy of the world.

Sources

This book is a concise history of the present century, the 20th century and centuries before that. All events described, took place and over the years, have become common knowledge. For as long as I can remember I have poured over newspapers, magazines and history books. Much of the material mentioned in this book is from the study of those events and from memory. I have lived through World War II, The Korean War, The Cuban Missile Crisis, the Assassination of President Kennedy, the historic journey of Apollo XI, The Vietnam War, The Cold War, the fall of the Berlin Wall and Communism, the expansion of NATO and now the Ukraine War. I also spent three years in West Germany during the height of the Cold War. At the American Checkpoint Charlie, I crossed the Berlin Wall into the Soviet Sector in East Berlin. It was a terrifying experience and almost didn't make it back. During World War II, India was an integral part of the British Empire. Two uncles of mine fought in North Africa under Field Marshall Montgomery against Field Marshall Rommel, the Desert Fox. India fought not only against Nazi Germany and Fascist Italy, but also against Imperial Japan in S.E. Asia. That infamous Bridge on the River Kwai brought the Imperial Japanese forces into Burma that threatened India – the Jewel in the British Crown. Relatives, friends and thousands of young men answered the call of duty and who, unfortunately never returned.

There is no person, my age and interested in history who has not heard or read of Neville Chamberlain who trusted Hitler and was betrayed, or the invasion of Poland that led to World War II, The massive invasion of the Soviet Union by Nazi Germany, the colossal failure of "Operation Barbarossa," the Yalta Conference, the division of Germany and Eastern Europe, the Cold War and the covert operations of the CIA. As students in a Catholic School, we were always told about the apparitions of the Blessed Virgin Mary with her anti-Russian message, the Miracle of the Sun and how evil Russia was – and still is and unless that country is converted and consecrated to Her Immaculate Heart, we are all doomed.

This book is meant to be concise, comprehensive, absorbing, thought-provoking, moving at a steady pace from one historical event to another, without plunging deeply into tedious details. It has been written with a fervent hope the reader would be motivated and encouraged to learn more and the role the Catholic Church played in those conflicts and events that shaped the world we live in today.

Acknowledgments

Heart-felt thanks to Clair of Creative Imagesetting for her bold and imaginative depiction of the book cover. And for her creation of the Dove of Peace.

This book could never have been completed without the help of my good friend, Alan Saunders. His incredible knowledge of computers greatly helped me – a person who is basically computer illiterate. To this kind, patient, loyal and steadfast friend, I offer my humble thanks.

I wish to thank the team at Friesen Press, my publisher, for their unsurpassed support, especially to Leah Erenberg. Her tough, no-nonsense approach, combined with her patience, kindness, understanding and guidance helped me get through the various stages of getting this book published.

Citation Information

Page 1. Britannica, T. Editors of Encyclopedia. "Wars of Religion" *Encyclopedia Britannica,* March 25, 2016. https: www.britannica.com/event/wars-of-religion.
Accessed Date: December 17, 2022.

Page 5. Britannica, T. Editors of Encyclopedia. "The Crimean War" *Encyclopedia Britannica,* October 7, 2022. https://www.britannica.com /event/Crimean-War.
Accessed Date: December 17, 2022.

Page 6. Bunting, T. "Charge of the Light Brigade" *Encyclopedia Britannica,* October, 18, 2022/
https://www.britannica.com/event/Charge-of-the-Light Brigade.
Accessed Date: December, 17, 2022

Page 6. Selanders, L. "Florence Nightingale." *Encyclopedia Britannica.*
https://wwws.britannica.com/ biography/Florence-Nightingale.
Accessed Date: December, 17,2022

Page 6. World Policy Journal. "Against Russophobia." Lieven, Anatol,
https://carnegieendowment.org/2001/01/01/"against-russophobia-pub-626
Accessed Date: December 27,2022.

Page 6. Becker, A. "Urban II" *Encyclopedia Britannica,* July 25, 2022.
https://www.britannica.com/biography/Urban-II.
Accessed Date: December 17,2022.

Page 7. Britannica, T. Editors of Encyclopedia. "Why is the Hagia-Sophia important. *Encyclopedia Britannica,* September 10, 2018.
https://www.britannica.com/question/Why-is-the-Hagia-sophia-important
Accessed Date: December, 17, 2022

Page 8. Madden, T. F. and Baldwin, Marshall, W. "Albigensian Crusade" *Encyclopedia Britannica,* May 5, 2010. https://britannica.com/event/Albigensian-Crusade
Accessed Date: December, 17, 2022

Page 8. Britannica, T. Editors of Encyclopedia, "Cathari" *Encyclopedia Britannica.* November, 25, 2022. https:/wwwbritannica.com/topic/Cathari
Accessed Date: December 17, 2022

Page 8. Hilderbrand, H.J., *Encyclopedia Britannica,* https://www.britannica.com/biography/The- Indulgences-Controversy Accessed Date: December 17, 2022.Accessed Date: December 17, 2022

Page 11. Britannica, T. Editors of Encyclopedia. "Our Lady of Fatima." *Encyclopedia Britannica,* July 20, 2022. https://britannica.com/event/Our-Lady-of-Fatima. Accessed: December 26, 2022.

Page 16. "Francisco Franco" Payne, S.G. *Encyclopedia Britannica.* November 16, 2022. https://www.britannica.com/biography/Francisco-Franco. Accessed Date: December 17, 2022

Page 19. Britannica, T. Editors of Encyclopedia . "Ustasa" *Encyclopedia Britannica,* November 1, 2015. https://www.britannica.com/topic/Ustasa Date Accessed: December 17, 2017

Page 20. Coppa, F.J. "Pius XII" *Encyclopedia Britannica,* October 5, 2022. https://www.britannica.com/biography/Pius-XII
Accessed: December 26, 2022
Gorsky, Johanthan. Yad Vashem. The World Holocaust Remembrance Center. https://yadvashem.org/articles/academic/pius-and-the-holocaust.html
Accessed Date; December, 17, 2022.

Page 23. Britannica, T. Editors of Encyclopedia. Lukas, J., Bullock, Baron, Wilfred, F. *Britannica Encyclopedia.* October, 4, 2022. https://www.britannica.com/biography/Adolf-Hitler
Accessed Date: November 26, 2022.

Page 25. Royde-Smith, J. Graham. "Operation Barbarossa." *Encyclopedia Britannica.* October 26,2022. https://www.britannica.com/event/Operation-Barbarossa.
Accessed Date: December 17,2022

Page 29. Marian Piety and the Cold War in the United Sates. The Catholic Historical Review. Vol. 72, no. 3, pp 403-24. JSTOR. https://www.jstor.org/25022337
Accessed Date: November 15, 2022

Page 29. Britannica, T. Editors of Britannica. Foot, J. and Hilbert, Christopher. "Benito Mussolini." *Encyclopedia Britannica."* September, 26, 2022. https: www.britannica.com/biography/Benito-Mussolini.
Date accessed: November, 24, 2022

Page 31. Britannica, T. Editors of Encyclopedia. Hingley, R. Francis. "Joseph Stalin." *Encyclopedia Britannica.* August, 24, 2022.
https://www.britannica.com/ biography/Joseph-Stalin
Accessed Date: November 27,2022

Page 31. Nicholas, H.G. "Winston Churchill." *Encyclopedia Britannica.* November, 26, 2022. https://www.britannica.com/ biography/Winston-Churchill
Accessed Date: November 30, 2022.

Page 31. Friedel, F. "Franklin D. Roosevelt." *Encyclopedia Britannica,* August 23, 2022. https://www.britannica.com/biography/Franklin-D-Roosevelt
Accessed Date: November 27, 2022

Page 31. Britannica, T. Editors of Encyclopedia. "Yalta conference" *Encyclopedia Britannica,* September 14, 2022. https://www.britannica.com/Yalta-Conference
Accessed Date: November 24, 2022

Page 34. Citation: C.N. Trueman. "Operation Unthinkable" historylearningsite.co.uk. The History Learning Site. 20 April,2015, 26 December 2022. April 20, 2015. https://historylearningsite.co.uk/world-war-two/world-war-two
Accessed Date: November 24, 2022

Page 37. Britannica, T. Editors of Britannica. "Russian Revolution." Encyclopedia. November 16, 2022. https://www.britannica.com/event/Russian-Revolution
Accessed Date: December 19, 2022.

Page 41. Britannica, T. Editors of Britannica. "French Revolution Key Facts." *Encyclopedia Britannica*. June 21, 2022. https://www.britannica.com/summary/French-Revolution-Key-Facts
Accessed Date: December 19, 2022

Page 44. Britannica, T. Editors of Encyclopedia. "Marshall Plan." *Encyclopedia Britannica*, November 24, 2022. https://www.britannica.com/event/Marshall-Plan
Accessed Date: December 13, 2022.

Page 44. Britannica, T. Editors of Britannica. "Cold War summary" *Encyclopedia Britannica*. April 29, 2021. https://www.britannica.com/summary/Cold-War
Accessed Date: December 19, 2022

Page 49. Britannica, T. Editors of Encyclopedia. "Vostok" *Encyclopedia Britannica*. July 23, 2018. https://www.britannica.com/technology/Vostok-Soviet-spacecraft.
Accessed Date: July 27, 2022.

Page 49. Britannica, T. Editors of Encyclopedia. "Yuri Gagarin" *Encyclopedia Britannica*, August, 26,2022. https://www.britannica.com/biography/Yuri-Gagrin
Accessed Date: November 27, 2022.

Page 51. Britannica, T. Editors of Encyclopedia. "Bandung conference." *Encyclopedia Britannica*. May 11, 2022. https://www.britannica.com/event/Bandung-Conference
Accessed Date: December 18, 2022

Page 52. Daily Mail. "Secret files reveal 9,000 Nazi war criminals fled to South America after World War II." Allan Hall for MAILONLINE. Published: 19 March 2012. Updated: 20 March, 2012. https://www.dailymail.co.uk/news/article-2117093/Secret-files-reveal-9-000-Nazi-war-criminals-fled
Accessed Date: December 20, 2022

Page 52. Britannica, T. Editors of Britannica. "September 30 Movement." Encyclopedia Britannica. November 18, 2016. https://www.britannica.com/event/September-30th-Movement.
Accessed Date: December 20, 2022.

Page 53. Others, F. Blackhouse and. "1953 Coup in Iran." *Encyclopedia Britannica.*
May 10, 2022. https:///www.britannica.com/event/1953-coup-in-Iran
Accessed Date: December 20,2022

Page 53. Britannica, The Editors of Encyclopedia. "Congo Free State." *Encyclopedia Britannica.* 27 Sep.2022. https://www.britannica.com/place/Congo-Free-State
Accessed Date: December 20, 2022

Page 55. Britannica, T. Editors of Encyclopedia. "Salvador Allende summary" Encyclopedia Britannica. July 24, 2021. https://www.britannica.com/summary/Salvador-Allende
Accessed Date: December 20,2022.

Page 57. Britannica, T. Editors of Encyclopedia. "Indochina wars." *Encyclopedia Britannica.* February 28, 2020. https://www.britannica.com/place/Indochina.
Accessed Date: December 13, 2022.

Page 58. Britannica, T. Editors of Encyclopedia. "Domino theory." *Encyclopedia Britannica,* January 28, 2022. https://britannica.com/ topic/domino-theory
Accessed Date: December 18,2022

Page 58. Manchester, William. "John F. Kennedy" Encyclopedia Britannica. November 8, 2022. https://www.britannica.com/biography/John-F. Kennedy
Accessed Date: December 20,2022

Page 61. Spector, R.H. "Vietnam War" Encyclopedia Britannica. November 30, 2020. https://www.britannica.com/event/Vietnam-War
Accessed Date December 28, 2022

Page 61. Britannica, T. Editors of Encyclopedia. "Ngo Dinh Diem" *Encyclopedia Britannica.* October 29, 2022. https://www.britannica.com/biography/Ngo-Dinh-Diem
Accessed Date: December 20,202

Page 67. Britannica, T. Editors of Encyclopedia. "Berlin Wall." *Encyclopedia Britannica.* November 13, 2022. https://www.britannica. com/topic/Berlin-Wall
Accessed Date; December 18, 2022

Page 68. Standoff in Berlin, October 1961. Hendrix, Thomas. L. U.S. Army Heritage and Education Center. October 22, 2010 https://www.army,mil/article/46993/standoff_in_berkin_october_1961
Accessed Date: December 18,2022

Page 69. Britannica, T. Editors of Encyclopedia." Cuban Missile Crisis" *Encyclopedia Britannica,* October15, 2022. https://www.britannica.com/event/Cuban-missile-crisis.
Accessed Date: November 27, 2022

Page 71. Wallenfeldt, Jeff, "Assassination of John. F. Kennedy" *Encyclopedia Britannica.* https://www.britannica.com/event/assassination-of-John-F-Kennedy
Accessed Date: November 27, 2022.

Page 71. Gibney, F. B. "Nikita Khrushchev" *Encyclopedia Britannica.* Sept. 7, 2022. https://www.britannica.com/biography/Nikita-Sergeyevich-Khrushchev
Accessed Date: November 27, 2022

Page 74. Hudson, Myles. "Wounded Knee Massacre" Encyclopedia Britannica. December 22, 2021.
https://www.britannica.com/event/Wounded-Knee-Massacre.
Accessed: December, 21, 2022.

Page 77-83. Britannica, T. Editors of Encyclopedia. "Apollo XI" *Encyclopedia Britannica.* October 19, 2022. https://www.britannica.com//topic/Apollo-XI
Accessed Date; November 27, 2022

Page 85. Britannica, T. Editors of Encyclopedia. "My Lai Massacre." Encyclopedia Britannica. April 29, 2021.
https://www.britannica.com/summary/My-Lai-Massacre.
Accessed: Dec. 22, 2022.

Page 85. Wallenfeldt, J. "Kent State Shooting" *Encyclopedia Britannica*, April 27, 2022. https://www.britannica.com/event/Kent-State-shooting.
Accessed Date: December 21, 2022

Page 86. Grenada. Swift, J. "U.S. Invasion of Grenada." *Encyclopedia Britannica."* October 18, 2022. https://www.britannica.com/event/ U-S-invasion-of-Grenada
Accessed Date: December 14, 2022

Page 89. Ray, M." Ukraine Crisis." Encyclopedia Britannica," August 16,2022. https://www.britannica.com/topic/Ukraine-crisis.
Accessed Date: December 22,2022

Page 90. Ray, M. "Viktor Yanukovych" Encyclopedia Britannica, July 5, 2022.
https://www.britannica.com/biography/Viktor-Yanukovyc
Accessed Date: December 22,2022

Page 93. Britannica, T. Editors of Encyclopedia. "Anschluss." *Encyclopedia Britannica.*
September 10,2022. https://www.britannica.com/event/Anschluss.
Accessed Date: December 22, 2022

Page 94. Britannica, T. Editors of Encyclopedia. "Reinhard Heydrich summary" *Encyclopedia Britannica*, May 20,2020 https://www.britannica.com/summary/ Reinhard-Heydrich
Accessed Date: December 21,2022

Page 94. Berenbaum, M. "Kristallnacht." *Encyclopedia Britannica*, November 2, 2022.
https://www.britannica.com/event/Kristallnacht. Accessed Date: December 26, 2022

Page 102. Britannica, T. The Editors of Encyclopedia. "Appeasement." *Encyclopedia Britannica,* January 8, 2022, https://www.britannica.com/ topic/appeasement-foreign-policy.
Accessed Date: December 14, 2022

Page 102. Britannica, T. Editors of Encyclopedia. "Sudetenland" *Encyclopedia Britannica,* October 13, 2022 https://www.britannica.com/place/Sudetenland
Accessed Date: December 14, 2022

Page 103. Britannica, T. Editors of Encyclopedia. "NATO summary" *Encyclopedia Britannica.* February 22, 2022. https://www.britannica.com/summary/North-Atlantic-Treaty-organization
Accessed Date: December 22, 2022

Page 103. Britannica, T. Editors of Encyclopedia. "Warsaw Pact." *Encyclopedia Britannica.* October 27, 2022. https://www.britannica.com/event/ Warsaw-Pact
Accessed Date: December 22, 2022

Page 109. Dr. Kissinger says Ukraine should cede territory to Russia to end war.
https://www.washingtonpost.com/world/2022/05/24/henry-kissinger-ukraine-russia-terrotory-davos. Timothy Bella. May 24, 2022
Accessed Date: December 22, 2022

Page 111. Britannica, T. Editors of Encyclopedia. "Vladimir Putin." *Encyclopedia Britannica.* December 12, 2022. https://www.britannica.com/biography/Vladimir-Putin
Accessed Date: December 22, 2022

Page 113. Britannica, T. Editors of Encyclopedia. "bombing of Dresden." *Britannica Encyclopedia.* November 24, 2022. https://www.britannica.com/event/bombing-of-Dresden
Accessed Date: December 21, 2022

Page 120. Zelazko, A. "Amanda Gorman" *Encyclopedia Britannica.* March 3, 2022. https://www.britannica.com/biography/Amanda-Gorman
Accessed Date: December 21, 2022

Page 123. Britannica, T. Editors of Encyclopedia. "Francis I summary" *Encyclopedia Britannica.* https://www.britannica.com/summary/Francis -I-pope
Accessed Date: December 21, 2022

Page 136. Britannica, T. Editors of Encyclopedia. "Bill Clinton" Encyclopedia Britannica. August, 23, 2022. https://www.britannica.com/biography/Bill-Clinton
Accessed Date: December 22, 2022.

Photo Credits

Page 7, Photograph of Blue Mosque in the city of Istanbul by Erika Patterson.

Page 11, Photograph of the sun by the author.

Page 47, Photograph of the moon by the author.

Page 79, "Apollo XI Blast-off" Photographs, courtesy of National Aeronautics and Space Administration. Printed in the U.S.A. Signed by astronaut Eugene Cernan during his visit to Vancouver, Canada for the Vancouver 2010 Winter Olympics and placed in author's Apollo XI scrapbook.

Page 82, "Eagle Leaves Moon Safely" Photographs, courtesy of National Aeronautics and Space Administration. Printed in U.S.A. and placed in author's Apollo XI scrapbook.

Page 83, "Apollo XI Astronauts" Photographs, courtesy of National Aeronautics and Space Administration. Printed in U.S.A. Signed by astronaut, Buzz Aldrin during his visit to Vancouver, Canada for the Vancouver 2010 Winter Olympics and placed in author's Apollo XI scrapbook.

Page 93, Photograph of a landscape of Austria by Ivana Michael.

Page 101, Photograph of the Vitus Cathedral in Prague by the author.

Endnotes

1 "Religious Wars" Inquisition. History.com Editors. Website Name: History.

https://www.history.com/topics/religion/inquisition Access: December 29, 2022.Publisher: A & E Television Networks. Last Updated: February 11, 2022. Original Published Date: November 17, 2017

Sources:

God's Jury: The Inquisition and the making of the modern world.
Cullen Murphy

Inquisition. University of Notre Dame

The Spanish Inquisition: Cecil Roth

2 "The Crimean War" Britannica, T. Editors of Encyclopedia. "What led to the Crimean War?" *Encyclopedia Britannica.* November 30, 2021. https://www.britannica.com/question/What-led-to-the-Crimean-War

Accessed: December 29, 2022

Britannica, T. Editors of Encyclopedia. "What was the outcome of the Crimean War?" *Encyclopedia Britannica,* November 30, 2001. https://www.britannica.com/question/What-was-the-outcome-of-the-Crimean-War

Accessed: December 20, 2022

3 "Against Russophobia." World Policy Journal. Lieven, Anatol. January, 01, 2001. Carnegie Endowment for International Peace. Accessed Date: November 16, 2022

"How the image of a besieged and victimized Russia came to be ingrained in the country's psyche." By Gregory Carleton. Published by The Conversation. Original article. April 18,2022. Accessed Date: November 16,2022

"Canada accused of stirring up mood of "Russophobia." National Post. December, 10, 2022. Russian ministry summoned Canada's ambassador in Moscow. In a statement, in a statement, it said Alison LeClaire, had

Been told Ottawa was "fomenting an atmosphere of "Russophobia." *Reuters.* Accessed Date: November 16, 2022

4 Pope Urban II orders first crusade. History.com Editors. Website Name: History.

https://www.history.com/this-day-in-history/pope-urban-ii-orders-first-crusade

Accessed: December 10, 2022. Publisher: A & E. Television Networks. Last Updated: November 22, 2022. Original Published Date: November 24, 2009

5 Hagia Sophia. History.com Editors. Website Name: History. https://www.history.com/topics/ancient-greece/hagia-sophia. Access Date: December 27,2022. Publisher: A & E. Television Networks. Last Updated: September 29, 2020. Original Published Date: January 12, 2008

Sources:

History. Hagia Sophia Museum

Allen, William. "Hagia Sophia, Istanbul. "Khan Academy

Matthews, Owen (2015) "Islamists and Secularists Battle Over Turkey's Hagia Sophia Museum." (Newsweek)

Hagia Sophia. Ancient History Encyclopedia

6 Krahenbuhl, Kevin. "The Albigensian Crusade. A Twist in the Story of the Crusades." Medieval Warfare 3, No. 4,(2013) : 6-11. https://www.jstor.org/stable/48578251. Accessed Date: December 28, 2022

7 Martin Luther and the 95 Theses. History.com Editors. Website Name: History.

https://www.history.com/topics/reformation/martin-luther-and-the-95-thesis. Access Date: December 28, 2022.

Publisher: A & E Television Networks. Last Updated: November 1, 2021. Original Published Date: October 29, 2009

8 Encyclopedia Britannica in 30 volumes. Macropedia. Knowledge in depth. Volume IV, Page 64.

"On October 13, 1917, a crowd generally estimated at 70,000 gathered at Fatima, witnessed a "miraculous solar phenomenon ...." Accessed: December 27, 2022

Apocalypse. "What happened at the miracle of Fatima. Silva, Lara. Portugal.com December 14, 2021 https:www.portugal.com/history-and-culture/what-happened-at-the-miracle-of Fatima

Accessed: December 27, 2022.

"Our Lady of Political Anxiety" JSTOR-Blackmore, Erin/May 12, 2017/https://daily.jstor.org/our-lady-of-political-anxiety. Accessed: December 27, 2022.

Cadegan, Una M. "The Queen of Peace in the shadow of War: Fatima and the U.S. Catholic Anticommunism." U.S. Catholic Historian 22, no.4(2004): 1-5. https://www..jstor.org/stable/25154930

Accessed Date; December 29, 2002.

9 The Red Scare. History.com Editors. Website Name: History. https://www. History.com/topics/cold-war/red-scare

Access Date: December 28, 2022. Publisher: A & E. Television Networks. Last Updated: February 28, 2020.

Original Published Date: June I, 2010

10 Spanish Civil War breaks out. History.com Editors. Website Name: History. Accessed: December 26, 2022.

https://www.history.com/this-day-in-history/spanish-civil-war-breaks-out. Publisher: A & E Television Networks.

Last Updated: July 16, 2020. Original Published Date: February 9, 2010

11 Adolf Hitler. History.com Editors. Website Name: History. Accessed: December 29, 2022. https://www.history.com/topics/worls-war-ii-/adolf-hitler-1 Last Updated: August 30, 2019. Publisher: A & E Television Networks. Original Published Date: October 29, 2009

Sources:

William L. Shirer, "The Rise and Fall of the Third Reich

IWonder -Adolf Hitler: The Man and the Monster, BBC

The Holocaust: A Learning site for Students, U.S. Holocaust Museum

12 Francisco Franco. History.com Editors. Website Name: History. Accessed Date: December 30, 2022.

https://www.history.com/topics/world-war-ii/francisco-franco Publisher: A & E Television Networks.

Last Updated: June 7, 2019. Original Published Date: November 9, 2009

13 Benito Mussolini. History.com Editors. Website Name: History. Accessed Date: December 30, 2022

https://www.history.com/topics/world-war-ii/benito-mussolin Publisher: A & E Television Networks

Last Updated: December 15, 2022. Original Published Date: October 29, 2009

Sources: Last 600 Days of Il Duce . Ray Mosley.

Mussolini. Jasper Ridley

Mussolini. Rupert Colley

Benito Mussolini (1983-1945) BBC

14 Jasenova concentration Camp. United States HolocaustMemorial Museum. "Introduction to the Holocaust." Holocaust Encyclopedia. https://encyclopedia.ushmm.org.content/en/article/introudction-to-the-holocaust

Accessed Date: December 29, 2022.

Goldstein, Ivo. "Croatia and Yugoslavia in the cleft between Totalitarianisms." *Zeitschrift fur Religious Und Geistesgeschichte* 69, no. 1(2017): 89-108. https://www.jstor.org/stable/44647369

Accessed Date: December 29, 2022

15 Britannica, T. Editors of Encyclopedia. "Pius XII summary" Encyclopedia Britannica, August 7, 2003.

https://www..britannica.com/summary/Pius-XII Accessed Date: December 30, 2022

Britannica, T. Editors of Encyclopedia. "Pius XII summary" Encyclopedia Britannica. https://www.britannica.com/biography/pius-xii/world war-ii-and-the-holocaust. Assessed Date: December 30, 2022

Pius XII and the Holocaust. Gorsky, Johnathan. https://www.yadvasham.org/articles/academic/pius-and-the-holocaust.html Website Title: Yad Vashem. The World Holocaust Remembrance Center. Accessed: Dec. 30, 2022.

Sources: Contributors: Carol Rittner

Stephen, D. Smith

Irena Steinfeldt

The Holocaust and the Christian World

Yad Vashem. 2000, pp. 133-137

16 Britannica, T. Editors of Britannica, "Operation Barbarossa." *Encyclopedia Britannica.* October 26, 2022

https: www.britannica.com/event/Operation -Barbarossa. Date Accessed November 24, 2022

17 Yalta Conference. History.com Editors. Website Name: History. Accessed Date: December 23, 2022.

https://www.history.com/topics/world-war-ii/Yalta-conference Publisher: A & E Television Networks

Last Updated: November 1, 2022. Original Published Date: October 29, 2009

18 Britannica, T. Editors of Encyclopedia. "Yalta Conference" Encyclopedia Britannica. September 21, 2022. https://www.britannica.com/topic/Cossack. Accessed: November 24, 2023.

19 Elliot, Mark. "The United States and the forced Repatriation of Soviet Citizens. 1944-47" Political Science Quarterly 88, no. 2(1993): 253-75. https://www. doi.org/10-2307/2149110. Accessed: February 24, 2023.

20 Churchill delivers Iron Curtain Speech. History.com Editors. Website Name: History. Accessed Date: December 23,2002. https://www.history.com/this-day-in-history/Churchill-delivers-iron-curtian-speech.

Publisher: A & E Television Networks. Last Updated: October 12, 2021. Original Published date: March 2, 2010.

21 Operation Unthinkable: Churchill's plan for World War III. April 28, 2014. Walker, Jonathan. Transcribed by Matthew, Version. November 2014. The National Archives, KEW, Richmond, TW94DU. Accessed: December 30, 2022. https://www.thehistory press.co.uk/articles/operation-unthinkable-Churchill's-plans-to-invade-the-soviet-union.

22 The Russian Revolution. History.com Editors. Website Name: History. Accessed Date: December 30, 2022

https://www.history.com/russia/russia-revolution Publisher: A & E Television Networks. Last Updated: July 28, 2022. Original Published Date: November 9,2009. Sources:

The Russian Revolution of 1917. Anna M. Cienciala, University of Kansas

The Russian Revolution of 1917. McGill University

The Russian Revolution of 1905. Marxist.org

The Russian Revolution of 1905. What were the major causes? Northeastern University

Timeline of the Russian Revolution. British Library

23 The French Revolution. History.com Editors. Website Name: History. Accessed Date: December 30, 2022

https://www.history.com/topics/france/french-revolution Publisher: A & E Television Networks. Last Updated: December 26, 2022. Original Published Date: November 9,2009. Sources:

French Revolution National Archives (U.K)

United States and the French Revolution, 1789-1799. Office of the Historian. U.S. Dept. of State.

Chateau de Versailles. Montecello.org

Proceedingss of the National Academy of Sciences.

Britannica, T Editors of Encyclopedia. "French Revolution. Key Facts. *Encyclopedia Britannica*. June 21, 2022.

https://www.britannica.com/summary/French-Revolution-Key-Facts. Assessed Date: December 30, 2022.

24 Cold War History. History.com Editors. Website Name: History. Accessed Date: December 30, 2022.istoryH

https://www.history.com/topics/cold-war/coldwar-history. Publisher: A & E Television Networks. Last Updated: December 06, 2022. Original Published Date: October 27, 2009.

25 Fear of Communism. Kselman, Thomas, A., and Avella, Steven . "Marian Piety and the cold war in the United States." The Catholic Historical Review, vol. 72, no. 3, pp 403-24. JSTOR.

https://www.jstor.org/stable/25022337. Accessed Date: December 30, 2022.

26 The Space Race. History.com Editors. Website Name: History. Accessed Date: December 23, 2022.

https://www.history.com/topics/cold-war/space-race. Publisher: A & E Television Networks. Last Updated:

February 23, 2022. Original Published Date: February 11, 2010.

27 Soviet cosmonaut, Yuri Gagarin becomes first man in space. History.com. Editors. Website Name: History. Accessed Date. December 30, 2022.. https://www.hitsory.com/this-day-in-history/first-man-in-space

Publisher: A & E Television Networks. Last Updated: April 8, 2020. Original Published Date: February 9, 2010.

28 The Bandung Conference concludes. History.com Editors. Website Name: History. Accessed Date: January 2, 2023. https://www.history.com/this-day-in-history/the-bandung-conference-concludes Publisher: A & E Television Networks. Last Updated: April 21, 2021. Original Date Published: November 13, 2009

Appadorai, A. "The Bandung Conference" India Quarterly 11, no.3(1955):207-35

https://www.jstor.org/stable/45068035 Accessed Date: January 2, 2023

29 Smith, Gaddis: "The Shadow of \john Foster Dulles" Foreign Affairs 52, no. 2 (1974):403-8.

https://doi.org/10.2307/20038056 Access Date: January 2, 2023

30 Scott, Peter Dale. "The United States and the Overthrow of Sukarno, 1965-1967" Pacific Affairs 58, no.2 (1985)

239-64. Https://doi.org/10.2307 2758262. Accessed Date: December 26, 2022

31 Kim Jaechun. "U.S. Covert Action in Indonesia in the 1960s: Assessing the motives and consequences" Journal of International and area studies 9. No 2(2002): 63-85. https://www.jstor.org/stable/43107065. Accessed: December 18, 2022.

32 How South America Became a Nazi Haven. History.com Editors. Website Name: History. Accessed Date: December 26, 2022. https:/www./history.com/news/how-south-america-became-a nazi-haven

Publisher: A & E Television Networks. Last Updated: August, 31, 2018. Original Published Date; November 12, 2015.

How top Nazi used 'ratline' escape route to flee to South America. https://www. Dailymail.co.uk/article-2099282/how-nazi-used-ratline-escape-route-flee-South-America Accessed Date: December, 26, 2022.

33 Gasioronski, Mark, J. "The CIA's TPBEDAMN Operation and the 1953 Coup in Iran" Journal of Cold War Studies 15, No. 4(2013): 4-24. https://www.jstor.org/Stable/26924362 Accessed Date. December 26, 2202.

34 Arfa, H. "Reza Pahlavi" Encyclopedia. Britannica Encyclopedia, January 10, 2023.https://www.britannica.com/biography/Reza Pahlavi. Accessed: February 18, 2023

35 Weisman, Stephen R, "What Really Happened in Cong: The CIA, the Murder of Lumumba, and the rise of MOBUTO" Foreign Affairs 93, no. 4(2014): 14-24. https://www.jstor.org/stable/24483553

Accessed Date: December 26, 2023.

36 Devine, Jack. "What Really Happened in Chile: The CIA Coup Against Allende, and the Rise of Pinochet" Foreign Affairs. 93, No. 4 (2014): 26-35 https://www.jstor.org/stable/2444483554.

Accessed Date: December 26, 2022.

37 Tonnesson, Stein. "The Longest Wars: IndoChina 1945-75" Journal of Peace research 22, no.1 (1995) 9-29.

https://www.jstor.org/stable/42 3583. Accessed Date: January 2,2023.

38 Kaufman, Barton I. "John F. Kennedy as World Leader: A Perspective on the literature." *Diplomatic History* - 17, no. 3 (1993): 447-69. https://www.jstor.org/stable/24912245. Accessed Date: January 2, 2023.

39 The Gulf of Tonkin Resolution. History.com Editors. Website Name: History. Accessed Date: January 2,2023

https://www. History.com/topics/Vietnam-war-gulf-of-tonkin-resolution-1 Publisher: A & E. Television Networks.

Last Updated: June 7, 2019. Original Published Date: October 29, 2009

Sources: The Truth about Tonkin. U.S. Institute.

U.S. Involvement in the Vietnam War: The Gulf of Tonkin and Escalation, 1964. U.S. State Department Office of the Historian

Statical Information about casualties of the Vietnam War. National Archives.

Vietnam War Casualties. Vietnam War/info.

Mass Atrocity Endings. Tufts.edu

40 Werner, Jayne, and Jessica M. Chapman. "Doomed from the Start? Ngo Dinh Diem and the start of the Vietnam War" *Diplomatic History* 39, no. 3(2015): 590-92. https://www.jstpor.org/stable/26376687.

Accessed Date: January 2, 2023

41 Article Title: Ngo Dienh Diem assassinated in South Vietnam. Author: History.com Editors. Website Name: History. Accessed: December 20, 2022. https://www.history.com/this-day-in-history/ngo-diem-assassinated-in-south-vietnam. Publisher: A & E Television Networks. Last Updated:October 30, 2019. Original Published Date: November 13, 2009.

42 Merritt, Richard L. *Review of The Berlin Wall. What was it all about?*, by Jack M. Schichk, Eleanor Lansing Hermann Zolling, Uwe Bahnsen, Gerhard Keiderling, Percy Stulz, Ernest F. Mueller, and Peter Greiner: *American Journal of Political Science* 17, no. 1 (1973): 189-95. https://www.doi.org/10.2307/2110483

Accessed Date: January 2, 2023

43 The standoff at Checkpoint Charlie.

Garthoff, Raymond L. "Berlin 1961: The Record Corrected." *Foreign Policy*, no. 84(1991): 142-56

https://www.doi.org/10.2307/10.2307/1148787 Accessed Date" January 2, 2023

44 Cuban Missile Crisis. History.com Editors. Website Name: History. Accessed Date: January 2. 2023

https://www.history.com/topics/cold-war/cuban-missile-crisis. Publisher" A & E Television Networks.

Last Updated: November 15, 2022. Original Published Date: January 4, 2010.

45 Medlin, William, K. "Khrushchev. A Political Profile IV" 10.2307/126295 The Russian Review 18, no.3, (1959): pp. 173-83 JSTOR. https://www.doi.org/10.2307/126295 Accessed Date: January 2, 2023Accesses

46 Kurtz, Michael, L. "The Assassination of John. F. Kennedy: A Historical Perspective" The Historian 45. No. 1

(1982): 1-19. https://www.jstor.org/stable/244445228. Accessed Date" January 2, 2023

47 Civil rights Movement. History.com Editors. Website Name: History. Accessed Date: Jan3, 2023

https://www.history.com/black-history/civil-rights-movement Publisher: A & E Television Networks.

Last Updated: January 18, 2022. Original Published Date: October 27, 2009

Sources:

A Brief History of Jim Crow. Constitutional Rights Foundation

Civil rights Act of 1957. Civil Rights Digital Library

Document for June 25th. Executive Order 8802. National Archives

Greensbro Lunch Counter Sit-In. African American Odyssey

Little Rock School Segregation (1957). The Martin Luther King Jr. Research and Education Institute Stanford

Rosa Marie Parks Biography. Rosa and Raymond Parks.

Selma, Alabama, (Bloody Sunday March 7, 1965) Black Past.org

The Civil Rights Movement (1919- 1960s) National Humanities Center

The Little Rock Nine. National Park Service US Department of the Interior. Little Rock Central High School, National Historic Site.

Turning Point. World War II. Virginia Historical Society.

48 Article title: Civil rights protesters beaten in "Bloody Sunday Attack" Author: History.com Editors. Website Name: History. https://www.history.com/this-day-in-history/bloody-sunday-civil-rights-protesters-beaten-selma. Accessed: March 07, 2023. Publisher: A & E Television Networks. Last Updated; January 11, 2023. Original Published Date; January 24, 2023.

49 Article Title: Fifteen-year-old Claudette Colvin refuses to give up her seat in a segregated bus. Author: History.com Editors. Website Name: History. https://www.history.com/claudette-colvin-refuses-to-give-up-seat. Accessed: March 02, 2023. Publisher: A & E Television Networks. Last Updated: January 24, 2023. Original Published Date: January 24, 2023.

50 US. Army massacres Sioux Indians at Wounded Knee. History.com Editors. Website Name: History.

https://www.history.com/this-day-in-history/u-s-army-massacres-indians-at-wounded-knee. Accessed Date: December 29, 2022. Publisher: A& E Television Networks. Last Updated: January 5, 2022. Original Published Date: November 24, 2009

45 Franco, Jere, "LOYAL AND HEROIC SERVICE: The Navahos and World War II. *The Journal of Arizona History* 27, no. 4(1986): 391-406. https: www.jstor.org/stable/41859701. Accessed Date: January 3, 2023.

52 Britannica, T. Editors of Encyclopedia. "Apollo XI" *Encyclopedia Britannica*, October 19,2022

https://www.britannica.com/Topic/Apollo-11 Date accessed: December 21, 2022

"Final Countdown begins for historic apollo" David Spurgeon. Globe and Mail. Toronto. Tuesday, July 15, 1969.

"Apollo coasting 250,000 miles to Moon." Robert Reguly. Toronto Daily Star. Wednesday, July 16, 1969.

"Heavens decided blast-off time should be 9.32. William Hines." Special to The Star. July 16, 1969. Chicago Sun-Times Service.

Dateline Moon. "A psalm of praise in Pope's handwriting wings to the moon." Toronto Daily Star. Friday, July 18, 1969.

"MAN ON MOON" Tranquility Base here. The Eagle has landed. Apollo XI Edition. The Globe and Mail. Toronto, Monday, July 21, 1969. New York Times and the Associated Press.

"A giant leap for Mankind" David Spurgeon and Terrance Wells. Globe and Mail Reporters. Toronto. July 21, 1969.

"$300,00 Suits protect moon men. Globe and Mail. Monday, July 21, 1969.

"The forgotten man waiting in the command ship." The Globe and Mail. Tuesday, July 22, 1969.

"Stop, give thanks." Aldrin tells world. Globe and Mail. Tuesday, July 22, 1969

"Congratulations from an ex-enemy." Globe and Mail. Tuesday, July 22, 1969

"Eagle leaves moon safely." Globe and Mail. July 24, 1969.

Photographs curtesy of National Aeronautics and Space Administration. Printed in U.S.A.

53 My Lai Massacre. History.com Editors. Website Name: History. Access Date: November 17, 2022.

https://www.history.com/topics/vietnam-war/mu-lai-massacre-1

54 Ryan, Bruce. "They Shoot Students, Don't They? The Australian Quarterly 42, no.3 (1970(: 10-13.

https://www. Doi.org/10.2307/20634367 Accessed Date" January 3, 20023.

55 Campbell, Horace. "THE AMERICAN INVASION OF GRENADA AND THE STRUGGLE IN THE CARRIBEAN." The Black Scholar 15, no.1 (1984): 2-7. https://www.jstor.org/stable/410167088.

Accessed Date: January 3, 2023.

Atique, Fauzia. "U.S. INVASION OF GRENADA." Pakistan Horizon 37,(1), 89-99. https://www.jstor.org/stable/414503910. Accessed Date: January 3, 2023.

56 Baker, Eugene C. "The Annexation of Texas" The South Western Historical Quarterly 50, no.1(1946): 49-74. https://www.jstor.org/stable/30237259. Accessed: March 02, 2023.

Article Title: the Americans overthrow Hawaiian Monarchy. Author: History.com Editors. Website Name: History. Accessed: March 03, 2023. Publisher: A & E Television Networks. https://www.history.com/this-day-in-history/americans-ovrthrow-hawaiian-monarchy. Last Updated: January 13, 2022. Original Published Date: February 07, 2010.

57 Britannica, T. Editors of Britannica. "Anschluss." Encyclopedia Britannica. September 1o, 2022.

https://www.britannica.com/event/Anschluss. Accessed Date: November, 26, 2022

58 Nazis launch Kristallnacht. History.com Editors. Website Name: History. Accessed Date: November 26, 2022

https://www.history.com/this-day-in-history/nazis-launch kristallnacht

Publisher: A & E. Television Networks. Last Updated: November 7, 2022. Original Published Date: November 24, 2009.

59 William, Samuel R. "The Origins of World War I. "The Journal of Interdisciplinary History," 18, no.4(1998): 795-818. https://www. doi.org/10.2307/204-825. Accessed: February 15, 2923.

60 Article Title: World War I. Author: History.com Editors. Website Name: History. https://www.history.com/topics/world-war-i-history. Publisher: A & E Television Networks. Accessed: February 15, 2023. Last Updated: January 12, 2023. Original Published Date: October 29, 2009.

61 MARENDY, PETER M. "Anti-Semitism, Christianity, and the Catholic Church: Origins, Consequences, and Responses." **Journal of the Church and State"** 47 no.2 (2005): 289-307. https://www.jstor.org/stable/23920986.

Accessed Date: January 04, 2023

Fischel, Jack. Review of THE CATHOLIC CHURCH AND THE HOLOCAUST, by Daniel Goldhagen. The Virginia Quarterly Review 79, no.4. (2003): 772-76 https://www. Jstor.org/stable/26440859

Accessed Date: January 4, 2023

Coppa, Frank J. "The 'silence' during the Holocaust." In The Life and Pontificate of Pope Pius XII, 152-73. Catholic University of America Press, 2013 https://www.doi.org/10.2307/j.ctt2jbm 59.11.

Accessed Date: January 6, 2023.

Kornberg, Jacques. "Pius XII and the Second World War: Poland" In The Pope's Dilemma: Pius XII Faces Atrocities and Genocide in the second world war, 141-55. University of Toronto Press, 2015.

https://www.jstor.org/stable/10.3138/j.ctvg2533p.8. Accessed Date: January 6, 2023.

62 Nazis Take Czechoslovakia. History.com Editors. Website Name: History. Accessed Date: November 17, 2022

https://www.history.com/this-day-in-history/ nazis-take-czechoslovakia Publisher: A & E Television Netwporks.

Last Updated: March 15,2022. Original Published Date: November 5, 2009.

63 Britannica, T. Editors of Britannica. "Neville Chamberlain" Encyclopedia Britannica. November 5, 2022. https://britannica.com/biography/Neville-Chamberlain Accessed Date: January 4, 2023

64 Mearsheimer, John J. "Why the Ukraine Crisis is the West's fault: The Liberal delusions that Provoked Putin." Foreign Affairs 93, no. 5(2014): 77-89. https://www. Jstor.org/stable/24483306. Accessed Date: January 5, 2023.

65 Cornelius, Deborah, S. "Hungary Enters the War" In *"Hungary in World War II*: Caught in the Cauldron," 146-81. Fordham University Press, 2011. https://doi.org/10.2307/j.ctt13Xo47.10 Accessed Date: January 5, 2023

66 Dr. Henry Kissinger, "Mission to Moscow: Clinton Must Lay the Groundwork for a New Relationship with Russia." Washington Post, May 15, 2000. Accessed Date: January 5, 2023.

67 Article Title: Americans hold Nazi rally in Madison Square Garden. Authors: History.com Editors. Website Name: History. Accessed Date: February 20, 2023. https://www.history.com/this-day-in-history/americans-hold-nazi-raly-in-madison-square-garden. Publisher: A & E Television Networks. Last Updated: January 19, 2022. Original Published Date: February 09, 2020.

68 Firebombing od Dresden. History.com Editors. Website Name: History. Accessed Date: December 21, 2022.

https://history.com/this-day-in-history/fireboming-of-dresden Publisher: A & E Television Networks. Last Updated: January 13, 2021. Original Published Date: November 5, 2009.

69 The siege of Leningrad. History.com Editors. Website page: History. Accessed Date" January 5, 2023.

https://www.history.com/this-day-in-history/seige-of-leningrad-begins Publisher: A & E Television Networks.

Lat Updated: September 2, 2020. Original Published Date: February 9, 2010.

70 Norman E.M., and Norman, Michael. "Bataan Death March" Britannica Encyclopedia. February 03, 2023 https://www.britannica.com/event/Bataan-Death-March. Accessed: March 27, 2023.

71 Brody H. Leonard SE, Nie JB, Weindling. U.S. responses to Japanese inhuman experimentation after World War II. Camb Q Health Ethics. 2014 Apr, 23(2):220-30. Doi:10.1017SO963180111000753. PMID:24534743; PMID: PMC4487829. FORMAT: NLM. Accessed: March 27, 2023

72 Article Title: The Rape of Nanking. Author: History.com Editors. Website Name: History. https://www.history.com/this-day-in-history/the-rape-of-nanking. Accessed Date: March 27, 2023. Publisher: A & E Television Networks. Last Updated: January 13, 2021. Original Published Date: November 05, 2009.

73 HENSMAN, SAVITI. "Pope Francis: Opening the Doors a Bit More" *Economic and Political Weekly*, 50, no. 4 (2015): 22-25. https://www.jstor.org/stable/24481539. Accessed Date: January 5, 2023.

Yuengert, Andrew M. "Pope Francis, His predecessors and the Market" *The Independent Review* 21, no. 3 (2017): 347-60. https://www.jstor.org/stable/26314740 Accessed Date: January 5, 2023.

Whaples, Robert M. "The Economics of Pope Francis: An Introduction," *The Independent Review*" 21, no. 3 (2017): 325-45. https://www.jstopr.org/stable/26314739 Accessed Date: January 5, 2023.

Aguilar, Mario I. "The Nation, the Poor and Others." In Pope Francis. His Life and Thoughts, 1st. ed., 132-57. The Lutterworth Press, 2014. https://www.doi.org/10.2307/j.ctt1gdz3p9. Accessed Date: January 5, 20

74 Kelly, Anthony, and Anthony J. Kelly. "Introduction" In Laudato Si: An integral ecology and the Catholic vision 1-8. ATF(Australia) Ltd. https://doi.org/10.2037j.ctv3wvw.

Accessed: December 21, 2022.

75 Holden, William N., and William Mansfield. "Laudato Si" A scientifically informed Church of the Poor confronts climate change" Worldviews 20, no. 1(2018):28-55. https://www.jstor.com/stable/ 26552298. Accessed" December 21, 2022

76 Communism Timeline. History.com Editors. Website Name: History. Accessed Date: January 5, 2023

https://www.history.com/topics/ Russia/communism-timeline. Publisher: A & E Television Networks.

Last Updated: January 18, 2022. Original Published Date: December 14, 2018

Sources:

"History of Communism," Stanford University.

Communism: Karl Marx to Joseph Stalin." Center for European Studies, University of North Carolina.

"From Tsar to USSR: Russia's chaotic year of Revolution." National Geographic.

"The Truman Doctrine, 1947," U.S. Department of State.

"The Chinese Revolution of 1949" U.S. Department of State.

"The Korean War Timeline," CBS News.

"Tiananmen Square Fast Facts" CNN

"United States Invades Grenada." Politico.

77 McCgwire, Michael. "NATO Expansion: A Policy of Error of Historic Importance" *Review of International Studies* 24. No. 1(1998): 23-42. https://www.jstor.org/stable/20097504. Accessed Date: January 5, 2023.

Jires. Jan. Review of *The Heyday of multilateralism*: Clinton Administration and NATO Enlargement, by Ronald D. Asmus. https://www.jstor.org/stable/23615866. Accessed Date: January 5, 2023.

78 McCwire, Michael. "NATO Expansion: A Policy of Historic Importance." Review of International Studies 24, no.1(1998):23-42. https://www.jstor.org/staable/20097504. Accessed: February 22, 2023.

Printed in the USA
CPSIA information can be obtained
at www.ICGtesting.com
JSHW021436280923
49288JS00002B/2/J

About The Author

Born, baptized and raised a Catholic, author Leslie Michael is, to this day, a practising Catholic. His life-long Catholicism led him to a deep interest in the teachings and politics of the Church. This ultimately got him especially invested in questions surrounding the "Miracle of the Sun" with its startling anti-Russian message. In addition, he desired to address the role of the Catholic Church in World War II and the cynical way it was used for religious, political and personal agendas.

His first book, "The Angel with a Broken Heart," published in 2010 is based on Ancient history. It vividly describes the incredible battle for heaven between Michael, the Archangel and the magnificent Lucifer, the "Bearer of Light" and the "Shining Star of Dawn." Having lost that battle and cast down from heaven, Lucifer, now Satan, vowed vengeance. The book is not about the goodness and mercy of God, but how cunning, diabolic and evil Satan is.